OPEN SOURCE
A Multidisciplinary Approach

Series on Technology Management

Series Editor: J. Tidd (Univ. of Sussex, UK)   ISSN 0219-9823

SERIES ON TECHNOLOGY MANAGEMENT – VOL. 10

OPEN SOURCE

A Multidisciplinary Approach

Moreno Muffatto

University of Padua, Italy

Imperial College Press

Published by

Imperial College Press
57 Shelton Street
Covent Garden
London WC2H 9HE

Distributed by

World Scientific Publishing Co. Pte. Ltd.
5 Toh Tuck Link, Singapore 596224
USA office: 27 Warren Street, Suite 401-402, Hackensack, NJ 07601
UK office: 57 Shelton Street, Covent Garden, London WC2H 9HE

Library of Congress Cataloging-in-Publication Data
Muffatto, Moreno.
    Open source : a multidisciplinary approach / by Moreno Muffatto.
      p. cm. -- (Series on technology management ; v. 10)
    ISBN-13 978-1-86094-665-3
    ISBN-10 1-86094-665-8
    Includes bibliographical references.
    1. Open source software. I. Title.

QA76.76.S46M95 2006
005.3--dc22

                         2006045782

British Library Cataloguing-in-Publication Data
A catalogue record for this book is available from the British Library.

Printed in Singapore

Preface

When I first came across the open source software phenomenon, I had no idea I would find it interesting enough to dedicate significant time and energy to writing a book about it. But I did, and in retrospect it's hard for me to say whether writing this book was more work or pleasure. The final product is a work, but writing it was certainly a pleasure. In some ways I've done what many programmers who voluntarily contribute to the development of open source software do: created something useful with a passion together with others who share the same interest.

The open source phenomenon basically started as a protest against proprietary commercial software and yet it is now under the widespread scrutiny of companies and governments. Millions of programmers make up the open source community, and universities, companies and governments around the world have become indirectly and directly involved in the phenomenon.

Why has open source software attracted all of this attention? Can it offer a new economically sustainable software development model? What are the social implications of this new model? Can it be exported to fields outside the software industry?

There is no doubt that the open source phenomenon has attracted attention because it brings together many of the other phenomenon that affect all of our lives daily: the digital revolution and economics of digital products, the controversies over intellectual property rights, the Internet, new ways of organizing the production of products and services, etc.. These phenomena bring up issues that can be studied from technological, economic, legal and sociological points of view.

Software is a digital product. There are certain characteristics of digital products that make them different from physical goods. Digital products are easy to copy and the results are as perfect as the originals. They are easy to transfer quickly to any part of the world, overcoming national borders, customs, etc. Finally, they can easily be modified to produce a new version of the original. Software is not the only product in the digital revolution. On the contrary, literary and artistic works, once they are put into digital format, take on the characteristics of digital products. The widespread evolution of digital products in many different fields has led to a heated debate on the protection of intellectual property.

Copyright and patent law were developed in an era when the products being invented were physical products and the works created were in a physical format. Clearly it becomes difficult to apply these laws in the same way to information goods and digital products. There have been two opposite reactions to this problem. On the one hand, the open source community has exploited copyright law and uses it to protect the freedoms to reproduce, modify and re-use software. On the other hand, commercial software companies are turning more and more to software patents to protect their intellectual property.

The open source community is not alone in promoting the philosophy of openness and free access. This philosophy is spreading to other areas of knowledge and human creativity and invention. New forms of intellectual property rights protection are being applied to music, photography, educational materials, etc., as is the case of the creative commons licenses. The basic idea behind this concept of openness is that sharing one's own work on the web not only offers greater opportunities for diffusion but for collaborating with peers on improving the work as well.

Internet potentially means the "death of distance", openness, freedom of access and expression, non-exclusiveness, no control, and democracy. Not all of these concepts have proven to hold true and, therefore, continue to be a sort of promise of what the Internet can still become. As the sociologist Manuel Castells has pointed out, the Internet was created in the context of a pre-existing need for being connected and for flexibility. The Internet is above all a tool for social communication. Many technologies are social constructions, but this is especially true in the case of Internet technology since its reach is so vast that it has become an extraordinary social phenomenon.

The Internet has also brought about new forms of production organization. As Castells has observed, though networks might be more flexible than bureaucratic organizations, they have also proved to be less efficient than centralized organizations in guaranteeing the coordination of production. In the past, networks were a privileged form of inter-personal relationships while organizations were responsible for production. Today networks have become more efficient thanks to the flexibility the Internet and new ICT tools offer. They are now able to manage greater complexity and they can work alongside a centralized organization in managing production.

What is most interesting about the open source phenomenon is the possibility it offers to "produce" a product in a way that is completely new and different from the way production traditionally takes place in a company. Eric Raymond, in his work *The Magic Cauldron*, says that "[t]o many people, the successes of the open-source community seem like an implausible form of magic. High-quality software materializes 'for free', which is nice while it lasts but hardly seems sustainable in the real world of competition and scarce resources". Products like the Linux operating system and Apache web server software have proved these "many people" wrong.

This completely different way of producing software inevitably leads to a series of questions and considerations regarding the evolution and transformation of our way of conceiving work organization, project organization and even company organization. The Information Revolution and development of networks have produced phenomena such as the growing connection between elements which are often extremely different from one another (computers, people, even smart objects). This has lead to phenomena which cannot be planned according to a top-down logic, but, on the contrary, "emerge" from interactions between elements and therefore "from the bottom". The approach most suitable for analyzing these phenomena is bottom-up thinking. With the development of information networks, and Internet in particular, it has been observed that not all phenomena which are developed can be designed and planned. In other words, networks involve social structures which make phenomena, to a certain degree, "emergent".

The way programmers in the open source community work may also lead us to re-think how we define work, or at least intellectual work. Their involvement in the open source community is voluntary and they dedicate their free time to doing the "work" of programming. The boundaries between work and pleasure are blurred. Linus Torvalds, the creator of the original Linux kernel, stated: "Linux was a hobby". Or in Raymond's words: "You need to care. You need to play. You need to be willing to explore". We could even go so far as to speak of a new work ethic based on passion, freedom, openness, and the social value of what one does.

In many ways, writing this book I too have been influenced by this new ethic. Like programmers in the open source community, writing this book has been a mix of work and play, and a job I have done with a great passion. Finally, again like the programmers, I hope to have made a useful and interesting contribution to the general community.

I did not embark on this journey alone. First of all, I must thank Matteo Faldani, co-author of a book in Italian on open source software (*Open Source. Strategies, organization, perspectives*, Il Mulino, Bologna, 2004). Matteo researched many of the more technical aspects of open source software that appear, in an updated version, in this book as well.

I would especially like to thank Sarah Guth, an ESL teacher at the University of Padua. She initially became involved in the project when I asked her to help me translate the book. However, she was soon affected by my own passion and enthusiasm. She proved to be a precious companion in this journey, helping me not only translate but better develop concepts that were still not clear in the book. She also helped me carefully check the facts and figures in this book doing her own research.

Finally, I must thank many of the students in my courses who over the past two years have contributed to the contents of this book with their suggestions, research and papers. I never could have completed the book without the precious help of these people. Nonetheless, I assume all responsibility for the contents in the book.

The open source phenomenon is still quite young and is changing and evolving at a very fast speed. Therefore, there is no way around the fact that some of the information in this book will become quickly outdated. Nonetheless, I hope that readers find the book useful and a stimulus for further research on this, what I consider to be, extremely interesting phenomenon.

Moreno Muffatto
University of Padua

Contents

Chapter 1

History of Open Source

1.1 Introduction

Open source software (OSS) is not a new concept. Although the term open source was coined just a few years ago, the concepts behind this particular way of developing software have existed since a long time. One of the pioneers in this field, Richard Stallman, remembers how software was developed several decades ago with these words:

> When I started working at the MIT Artificial Intelligence Lab in 1971, I became part of a software-sharing community that had existed for many years. Sharing of software was not limited to our particular community; it is as old as computers, just as sharing of recipes is as old as cooking. But we did it more than most.

This was not only the case at universities. In the 1960s, IBM and others sold their first large-scale commercial computers with free software. "Free" meant that the source code was free and available and, therefore, the software could be improved and modified. In other words, hardware was the product being sold, not software. By the mid-1970s this began to change. Software became a commercial proprietary product that could not be redistributed or modified. As a result of this change software could no longer be freely shared by programmers as it had been in previous times. Stallman was not happy with this evolution and wanted to take software development back to its former status by creating a new software sharing community. For this reason he left MIT. Several years later, he explained his choice to leave his post at MIT:

> In January 1984 I quit my job at MIT and began writing GNU software. Leaving MIT was necessary so that MIT would not be able to interfere with distributing GNU as free software. If I had remained on the staff, MIT could have claimed to own the work, and could have imposed their own distribution terms, or even turned the work into a proprietary software package. I had no intention of doing a large amount of work only to see it become useless for its intended purpose: creating a new software-sharing community.[1]

Stallman would probably have just been a visionary had others not latched on to his ideas obtaining unexpected results. This was the case, for example, of Linus Torvalds and his creation Linux. Torvalds himself was surprised by the success of Linux:

> Linux today has millions of users, thousands of developers, and a growing market. It is used in embedded systems; it is used to control robotic devices; it has flown on the space shuttle. I'd like to say that I knew this would happen, that it's all part of the plan for world domination. But honestly this has all taken me a bit by surprise. I was much more aware of the transition from one Linux user to one hundred Linux users than the transition from one hundred to one million users.[2]

What is even more noteworthy is that software developers and hackers were not the only ones interested in this new phenomenon. So-called *free software* also caught the attention of companies and institutions. The most surprising reaction was the fact that Microsoft saw free software, or what came to be defined as open source software, as a threat to its own business. In 1998, Microsoft carried out a careful study of open source software that was reported in a series of originally confidential documents that the open source community baptized the "Halloween Documents". In these documents Microsoft concluded the following:

In recent years, corresponding to the growth of Internet, OSS projects have acquired the depth & complexity traditionally associated with commercial projects such as Operating Systems and mission critical servers. Consequently, OSS poses a direct, short-term revenue and platform threat to Microsoft - particularly in the server space. Additionally, the intrinsic parallelism and free idea exchange in OSS has benefits that are not replicable with our current licensing model and therefore present a long term developer mindshare threat.

The Linux OS is the highest visibility product of the Open Source Software process. Linux represents a best-of-breed UNIX, that is trusted in mission critical applications, and - due to it's open source code - has a long term credibility which exceeds many other competitive OS's. Linux poses a significant near-term revenue threat to Windows NT Server in the commodity file, print and network services businesses.[3]

These documents made it clear that by 1998 the open source community had become more than just a large community of hackers developing software, but rather was beginning to pose a threat to one of the most important software company in the world.

Our journey into the world of open source software will begin with the history of the open source phenomenon. In this chapter we will take a look at the main historical events that mark steps in the development of the community and its products. The history of OSS can be divided into four main stages: the age of the pioneers, the beginnings of the open source movement, the diffusion stage and the institutionalization stage. Specific events define and characterize each stage and show how the attention given to this type of software and the importance it took on grew in each stage.

As I write this book, on the one hand OSS is becoming more and more diffused and on the other hand it is under the attack of lawsuits. Companies that use or support OSS are being brought to courts by those who want to defend the ways of developing and distributing proprietary software. The aim of these court cases is to reduce the momentum OSS has achieved in recent years.

1.2 The Age of Pioneers

In the sixties and seventies the knowledge and tools regarding information technologies and software development belonged to a small community of researchers. Software was developed at universities in close contact with the research laboratories of a few large companies. The software that was developed was distributed freely without any limitations, respecting academic traditions of sharing knowledge. In other words, software was considered, as was scientific research, to be a public good. Free access to research results was an essential characteristic of software that could not be renounced.

These researchers were able to collaborate thanks to a very important tool: Arpanet, the antecedent to Internet. This network linked the various communities developing software and facilitated the sharing of programs and knowledge. Sharing and exchange were what kept technological innovation in motion.

New software and hardware were developed at a very fast speed. However, fast development and the lack of any form of standardization meant that software products and computers were often incompatible. However, since these new software products needed to be tried out and used in very different operational settings, researchers had to deal with the boring and tiresome task of translating large amounts of software. Manual translation was the only way to achieve the best possible compatibility with each single system. In order to avoid wasting time translating, specific projects were undertaken to develop software that could be compatible with other software or hardware. The laboratories at Bell (AT&T) developed some software products that could easily be used on different hardware platforms.

The efforts to develop products that were universal and independent of the system being used involved developing programming languages as well. Programming languages are the basic tool used to write the codes that computers must interpret to execute any given task. In 1972, Dennis Ritchie developed a programming language called "C". C was a multi-platform language, or, in other words, it could be used regardless of the specific hardware or software. This language quickly became one of the most widely used instruments for developing software products and continues to enjoy a large user community today.

From 1969 to 1974, Ken Thompson and his team of researchers at Bell Labs Computing Research Department developed the first version of the Unix operating system. An operating system is "[t]he foundation software of a computer system, responsible for controlling and launching the installed applications and computer peripherals."[4] Unix was one of the first products to be developed using the C programming language and, as a consequence, was the first operating system to be developed with the aim of being usable regardless of the type of machine/computer it would be used on.

The source code of Unix was freely distributed during the seventies. The source code is the series of instructions written in a language that is easy for programmers to use, e.g. Unix's source code is written in C. Human-readable source code must then be translated by a compiler or assembler into the computer-readable object code in order to execute the instructions. By distributing Unix with the source code, Bell Labs effectively opened up the development of Unix to a wider community of researchers and programmers. In 1975, Ken Thompson spent a year as a visiting professor at the University of California-Berkeley. He took Unix with him and the University became involved in the development and debugging of Unix. The Berkeley Software Distribution (BSD) developed versions of Unix in parallel with Bell Labs versions of Unix. The first version of BSDUnix was released in 1979. This was covered by what may be considered one of the first open licenses guaranteeing use, modification and redistribution of the source code.

A fast, diffused and low-cost means of communication was still needed to allow researchers in various universities and laboratories to collaborate on software development projects. In 1973, Vinton Cerf and Bob Kahn, two researchers working with DARPA (The Defense Advanced Research Projects Agency of the US Department of Defense) created the foundations for what would become the Internet: the communication protocol TCP/IP (Transmission Control Protocol/Internet Protocol). The new protocol made it possible to connect the different computers in the network in a faster and more reliable way.

In 1979, Eric Allman, a student at the University of California Berkeley, developed Sendmail, a program for sending electronic mail over the Arpanet network. This program, which was free of any intellectual property constraints, quickly became the *de facto* standard for Arpanet and is still widely used for the Internet network.

Up to this point in our story, software was still considered to be a mere support tool for hardware, or, in other words, a tool needed to use and, above all, spread the use of computers. Therefore, only hardware had a commercial value whereas software was basically a freely distributed knowledge product. In the late 1970s, Unix was the only portable, machine-independent, affordable operating system. AT&T began to recognize the commercial value of this software product. In 1984, a provision of the Antitrust Division of the US Department of Justice forced AT&T to separate its software products from other products. AT&T decided to focus on producing, distributing and selling Unix as a commercial product. From this point on Unix became protected by property rights and was no longer available for free to development communities outside the company. Not even the academic research departments that had participated in the development of the Unix operating system were able to easily obtain new versions of the product.

In the early to mid eighties, the widespread diffusion of personal computers eventually lead to the transformation of software for personal computers from free products into commercial products. Since PC users usually did not have programming skills and depended on software to use computers, they were willing to pay for software, giving it a commercial value.

1.3 The Beginnings of the Open Source Movement

The most significant consequence of the birth of a market for software proved to be the migration of the best programmers from academic research centres to the R&D laboratories of private companies. For example, at the beginning of the eighties, the company Symbolics hired almost all of MIT's Artificial Intelligence Lab's programmers. This move marked the growth of a software market characterized by the protection of intellectual property. The researchers who stayed on at universities had to negotiate these property rights with companies in order to obtain executable copies of some important products. Many researchers who had, up to then, directly contributed to developing these products felt frustrated by these changes. Furthermore, commercializing software meant that it couldn't be freely distributed and for academic researchers this was considered to be an obstacle to scientific research and innovation. For there to be a free exchange of information and cooperation, there had to be free access to source codes. In academic development communities the fundamental values of freedom and collaboration had not changed. Companies, on the other hand, considered any form of software sharing to be on the same level as pirating software. Outsiders were not allowed to make any changes to software protected by copyright even if the change might actually have improved the product.

Frustration with the destruction of the academic development community lead Richard Stallman, then a researcher at MIT, to try to rebuild the community. Stallman wanted to change the socio-economic and legal system that was limiting software sharing. Therefore, his first aim was to oppose the software industry and the rules it applied to defend intellectual property. To do this, in 1984 Stallman started the GNU project ("GNU's not Unix") to develop a free-access operating system based on Unix with applications and development tools as well. To support the GNU project, the Free Software Foundation (FSF) was founded in 1985. The main aim of the FSF was to redevelop a series of products based on the concept of free software. For the FSF, the word "free" meant "freedom", i.e. the possibility to use programs, modify source codes and then distribute the modified versions. The word "free" did not, therefore, mean "free of charge" but rather "free access". Stallman himself clearly explained this concept: "The term free software has nothing to do with price. It is about freedom". In other words, the aim of the FSF was to protect free software from being appropriated by others and used for commercial ends.

The first problem that the Free Software Foundation had to face was that, at the time, there were no software licenses that could actually protect free access and free use. The aim of licenses is to describe in detail what can and cannot be done by software programmers and users. In 1988, the FSF published the first version of the General Public License (GPL) which introduced the concept of "copyleft". The concept of copyleft opposes the concept of copyright. Rather than protecting a product's property rights, copyleft protects the freedom to copy, distribute, and change a product. As Stallman explained:

> The goal of GNU was to give users freedom, not just to be popular. So we needed to use distribution terms that would prevent GNU software from being turned into proprietary software. The method we use is called "copyleft." Copyleft uses copyright law, but flips it over to serve the opposite of its usual purpose: instead of a means of privatizing software, it becomes a means of keeping software free.[5]

And the preamble to the GPL states:

> …[t]he licenses for most software are designed to take away your freedom to share and change it. By contrast, the GNU General Public License is intended to guarantee your freedom to share and change free software--to make sure the software is free for all its users.[6]

The General Public License had a strong influence on the development community because it laid down clear rules protecting the freedom of projects developed by the Free Software Foundation. Furthermore, the license proved that there was an alternative model for software development which strongly opposed the commercial view of companies. A community of voluntary software developers, the so-called hacker community, grew around the FSF and GPL. However, the GNU project, which mainly focused on developing a free operating system, still depended too much on the Unix code. In order to be freed up from the Unix constraint, a free version of the kernel had to be developed. A kernel is the heart of an operating system that controls memory, disk, process and task management.

In 1990, a computer science student at the University of Helsinki, Linus Torvalds, started to carefully study the Unix operating system. Torvalds had a general interest in the kernels of operating systems and in particular in multi-tasking techniques. His choice to study Unix depended on the fact that DOS (Microsoft), a more accessible and less expensive operating system, did not implement multi-tasking. At that time Unix was still relatively expensive and a student could certainly not afford it. Furthermore, the University of Helsinki could not afford to buy enough computers using Unix for all its students. Torvalds spent much of his time waiting for a computer to free up in the University's computer labs and found this annoying and frustrating. Therefore, he decided to work on developing his own Unix-like operating system. He had no idea how he would manage such a big project, but decided to give it a try anyway. Torvalds did not have the resources, time, tools or skills to develop an operating system on his own. His inexperience and inability to realistically evaluate the effort required actually proved to be an important factor in the starting up and success of the project. Torvalds himself later said that had he fully understood the efforts required to carry out the project he never would have started in the first place.

His efforts initially focused on studying Minix, a Unix clone, developed for didactic purposes by Andrew Tanenbaum at the University of Amsterdam. Torvalds did not plan on developing the whole kernel. In fact, much of his work at the beginning focused on developing some simple task-switching programs, i.e. the multi-tasking that had originally got him interested in operating systems. Torvalds diffused the news of his project in an online newsgroup with the following message on August 25, 1991:

Hello everybody out there using minix – I'm doing a (free) operating system (just a hobby, won't be big and professional like GNU) for 386(486) AT clones. This has been brewing since April, and is starting to get ready. I'd like any feedback on things people like/dislike in minix, [...] I'd like to know what features most people would want. Any suggestions are welcome, but I won't promise I'll implement them.[7]

Within the following month, Torvalds managed to develop a stable version of his product, which he decided to call Linux (Linus+Unix). This first version of the kernel included a simple and primitive file system but it was still incomplete. Once again, he called on the on-line community for its indispensable collaboration in helping the project evolve into a more complete form. To get help from this virtual community, Torvalds posted another message about his project on October 5, 1991, explicitly asking for help in developing his kernel. The announcement by Linus Torvalds was accompanied by this message:

> I'm working on a free version of a Minix look-alike for AT-386 computers. It has finally reached the stage where it's even usable (though it may not be, depending on what you want), and I am willing to put out the sources for wider distribution.... This is a program for hackers by a hacker. I've enjoyed doing it, and somebody might enjoy looking at it and even modifying it for their own needs. It is still small enough to understand, use and modify, and I'm looking forward to any comments you might have. I'm also interested in hearing from anybody who has written any of the utilities/library functions for minix. If your efforts are freely distributable (under copyright or even public domain) I'd like to hear from you so I can add them to the system. [8]

The response to Torvalds's message was immediate and extraordinary. A large community began to develop around the Linux project. By this time, the internet was becoming more and more diffused making the development and expansion of an online community of software developers possible. The increase in the size of the community automatically lead to an increase in productive capacity both in terms of number of projects that could be developed and the quality of the products.

Collaboration between the Linux community and the Free Software Foundation lead to the development of GNU-Linux, a complete non-commercial operating system. GNU-Linux would prove to be one of the most extraordinary results created by a community of voluntary software developers. [9]

The work carried out by the community made it possible for Torvalds to release the first official version of the Linux operating system in 1994. During the first few years of development, the growth of the operating system was exponential; the code lines that made up Linus went from the 10,000 developed by Torvalds to 1.5 million lines in 1998. This project, which had been started to satisfy the curiosity of one single person, had managed to involve 12 million users and 120 different countries. Today Linux is one of the few free products in direct competition with an already established proprietary product, Microsoft's Windows operating system, that has managed to widen its own market share.

1.4 Diffusion

Following the rapid development of the GNU-Linux system, some companies began to get involved in the project by using it and/or contributing to its development. In 1994, Bob Young and Mark Ewing founded Red Hat with the aim of improving some of the main drawbacks to Linux, namely to create a more user-friendly interface and increase the number of application programs that could be used with this new operating system.[10] Red Hat provides technical assistance, documentation and training and develops more user-friendly configurations to distribute Linux to non-expert users.

Red Hat is one of the most important companies involved in the development of software products in a copyleft context. Red Hat is a so-called *pure player*, i.e. a company whose business model is completely focused on deploying a copyleft product and related services. Only a fraction of the company's profits come from the direct sale of software packages and the value of these packages does not depend on the cost of the individual products but rather the cost of integrating the products and packaging them. The result is that the products Red Hat deploys are much cheaper than other software packages built around proprietary software products. At the same time, anyone can copy and distribute Red Hat products for free since they are protected by copyleft.

Red Hat follows the evolution of the Linux operating system very closely. Every time Torvalds and his collaborators distribute a new version of the kernel, Young and Ewing take advantage of the new release to build a more complete and operational software package based on it. Red Hat's aim is to complete the Linux platform by adding and integrating the necessary tools and most useful application programs. These additions are made in order to make the operating system actually usable for a non-expert clientele and, as a consequence, to promote the mass diffusion of Linux.

By 1999, Red Hat had proved so successful that in one of the US Justice Department's various antitrust cases against Microsoft, the software giant used Red Hat's Linux system as proof that it did not have a monopoly on the operating system market. Microsoft basically involuntarily publicized and legitimized Linux and Red Hat. Red Hat then decided to widen its market by going abroad, first to Europe and then to Asia. It now occupies a significant share of the Chinese market.

In 2001, Red Hat proposed a solution to one of the numerous antitrust cases by the US Justice Department against Microsoft. The solution was that the government allow Red Hat to provide the Linux operating system, office application programs and many other products for free to all American schools, private and public. In exchange, Microsoft would have to provide the necessary computers. The aim of this proposal was not to save Microsoft from being found guilty, but rather to deploy non-proprietary products in every school district in the United States. Obviously Microsoft's managers understood Red Hat's real intentions and did not accept the offer. In fact, the proposal was an attempt to open school districts to non-proprietary software and by accepting the proposal Microsoft would have risked losing its control over the market. In other words, had Microsoft accepted this solution, students and, therefore, future generations of computer users would have grown up knowing how to use non-proprietary products rather than Microsoft products. Bill Gates and the managers at Microsoft decided to face the antitrust case and the possible consequences it might have considering even a heavy fine to be the lesser of the two evils.

In reality, the use of non-proprietary products and Red Hat Linux in particular is already widespread in many universities. North Carolina State University was the first in a series of universities to make an agreement with Red Hat for the supply of products to its Engineering

Departments. Red Hat's aim is to deploy these products in all schools in order to free educational institutions from the influence of proprietary products and standards. The idea is, therefore, to establish the Linux operating system, and in general non-proprietary software, as alternative standards.

As the Linux project grew, so did another project for a free product: the web server software Apache. In 1994, a group of programmers in the California Bay Area formed the Apache Group to develop a free, reliable web server. By December 1995 the group had developed and was able to release Apache 1.0. Apache had immediate success and quickly became the most popular HTTP server on the Internet. In 1999, the members of the Apache Group formed the Apache Software Foundation (ASF) to provide organizational, legal and financial support for the Apache web server.[11]

1.5 Institutionalization

During the mid-nineties, members of the various free software development communities began to feel the need to overcome the misunderstandings the word "free" was causing among many users. A group of programmers, many of whom had built up their reputations within the Free Software Foundation, began to work together to try and find a strategy to make the concept of free software more appealing to companies. The aim of this initiative was to avoid the widespread association of the word "free" with the meaning "free of charge". The Free Software Foundation had tried to disassociate itself from this interpretation by using the motto "free speech, not free beer". The Free Software Foundation's mission was to promote the freedom of information and research, not to destroy the commercial value of software. This misinterpretation of the word "free" was the weak point of the free software philosophy and kept many software companies from becoming involved in the community. In order to change this, companies had to believe that involvement in the free software development company had something to offer them as well.

In 1997, at a Linux Congress, Eric S. Raymond presented a paper called "The Cathedral and The Bazaar". This paper compared the commercial software development model (the cathedral) to the new development model based on a community of dispersed software developers and on the free distribution of codes (the bazaar). Raymond proposed the use of the term "open source" as the best alternative to "free". This paper marked the beginning of the study of voluntary development communities, their behaviours and the economic sustainability of this model.

1998 was a very important year in the history of the open source community and open source software. The "open source" label was decided on during a strategy session in February 1998 that included several members of the Linux community and Raymond himself. In the same month Bruce Perence and Eric Raymond founded the Open Source Initiative (OSI)[12] with the main aim of creating a document that would precisely define open source software (The Open Source Definition).[13] In April of the same year, the OSI officially approved the term "open source" to indicate the accessibility, efficiency, reliability, flexibility and innovation that would characterize open source software.

The new definition managed to make free software much more appealing to companies even if the Free Software Foundation and the Open Source Initiative did not have the same philosophy and did not agree on the methods of software development. Regardless of these differences, however, the majority of open source projects were originally supported by and developed in collaboration with the Free Software Foundation.

On January 23, 1998, an announcement was made that surprised everyone in the IT world: Netscape intended to make the source code of its browser Navigator public, i.e. to share it with the open source development community.[14] Netscape Navigator was quickly losing market share to its main competitor Microsoft Explorer. Consequently, Netscape made the difficult decision to open Navigator's source code and started a project called Mozilla. The announcement created a lot of interest within the open source community and especially among the main supporters of the Open Source Initiative and the Free Software Foundation.

Netscape's group of managers had to face a series of very challenging problems. First of all, the property of some parts of Navigator were shared with other companies. Therefore, Netscape had to communicate its change in strategy and, if possible, convince the partner companies to support the Mozilla project. Netscape set a deadline, February 24, 1998, by which each partner had to communicate its decision. They could choose to participate in the Mozilla project or leave it. Since some companies backed out, Netscape had to eliminate some code.

Another problem Netscape had to deal with was what license to choose to best respect the aims of the project. Mozilla needed a license that would motivate the community of volunteers to contribute to the project and at the same time protect the economic interests of Netscape. None of the licenses that existed at that time, including the open source licenses, met these requirements. Therefore, on March 5, 1998, Netscape proposed a new license created by the company itself. The license, called the Netscape Public License (NPL), was immediately presented to the open source community for feedback. Unfortunately, the reaction of the community was very negative. The community did not like the presence of some norms that reserved Netscape some special rights. One of these was the possibility Netscape would have to not share with the community some of the parts of the new code developed as a part of the Mozilla project. Netscape, believing the support of the entire open source community to be indispensable to the success of Mozilla, tried to remedy the situation. The license was reviewed and modified and on March 21, 1998 Netscape proposed a second license called the Mozilla Public License (MPL). This license was different from the NPL in that it did not reserve Netscape any particular privileges. The community accepted the MPL. This new license convinced the open source community that the Mozilla project was serious and credible.

The official presentation of the project was quite unique. The location had to attract the curiosity of the community of developers, which is notoriously made up of anti-conformist and eccentric hackers. A party, open to all, to celebrate the project was held on April 1, 1998 in one of the biggest nightclubs in San Francisco. Netscape wanted the substantial and credible involvement of the open source community. The success of the Mozilla project was considered to be directly related to the ability of the company to obtain the consensus and contribution of the best programmers in the community. Netscape had to move fast. The fact that Netscape was the first major company to take part in the open source community was one of the greatest advantages the Mozilla project gave Netscape.

Netscape wanted to be responsible for managing the Mozilla project and so, on May 24, 1998, it registered the domain mozilla.org. A series of support tools for the development community were provided on this site. Netscape wanted to play an active role in the decision making process and, therefore, had to create an efficient structure around Mozilla. At the same time, however, this structure had to be separate from the rest of the company. Netscape had to make a significant effort to reach a compromise between influencing the project and allowing the development community the freedom it needed. At the end of this initial planning stage, Netscape was finally able to state: "the lizard [Mozilla] is free".[15]

Following the foundation of the Open Source Initiative and the beginning of the Mozilla project, hundreds of open source projects were started and numerous companies began to directly participate in the development and diffusion of these projects. For example, in 1999 IBM announced that it wanted to use the Linux operating system and Apache web server in its e-business solutions. Other companies followed IBM's example and began to become directly or indirectly involved in the open source community. For example, in the same year Sun Microsystems launched a project to share the development of its own office product, StarOffice, with the open source community. This lead to the development of OpenOffice.org, an open source office project and product. OpenOffice.org is a complete office suite with features comparable to Microsoft Office features.

The involvement of companies validated open source concepts and strategies. Companies in the IT industry were forced to start comparing their own business model to open source software development. Even Microsoft, regardless of its position on the market, had to begin to carefully evaluate the open source phenomenon and study strategies to effectively respond to the threat it posed. In fact, the "Halloween Documents" already mentioned at the beginning of the chapter, indicated that Microsoft considered Linux to be a real threat to its own business model. Microsoft eventually announced its intention to release part of the source code of some of its proprietary software products exclusively to some governments and institutions.

Table 1.1 shows the main events that played a role in the creation and evolution of open source software.

Table 1.1 – Significant historical events in the development of the open source software.

1968	Arpanet
1969	First version of Unix
1972	"C" language
1973	TCP/IP
1979	Sendmail AT&T starts selling Unix BSD first version
1984	GNU project is launched
1985	Free Software Foundation is launched
1991	Linux Project is launched
1994	Red Hat is founded
1995	Apache Software Foundation is launched
1998	Open Source Initiative is founded Mozilla Project is launched
2000	Linux included in IBM products Sun launches Open Office
2003	Microsoft first announcement of limited access opening of parts of Windows EU-IDA publishes Open Source Software guidelines for Governments The city of Munich announces Open Source Software adoption
2004	French Government announces large scale migration to Open Source Software (ADELE)

Thanks to the open source movement, the development model that had been developed within the context of the Free Software Foundation found new outlets. The way the Open Source Initiative interpreted this model made it possible to involve companies in open source projects, favouring the diffusion of open source products on the market. This stage in the evolution of open source software saw the creation of an efficient network of companies involved in offering support services for open source products and products complementary to open source software. Furthermore, some governments and public administrations began to show interest in the community and its products. Some governments are currently considering the possibility of using open source software in place of proprietary software to manage public information. Governments manage large quantities of information, deal with the public and have legislative power. All of these factors make the idea of government involvement in the open source community very appealing to programmers

1.6 Recent Developments

The open source phenomenon has led to the creation of free, open software products that can compete with proprietary products on the market. It has also introduced a new way of developing software. However, the success of both open source products and the open source model have made the open source community the object of many legal attacks. The aim of these attacks is to limit the diffusion of open source software.

On March 7, 2003 the SCO Group filed a $1 billion lawsuit in the US against IBM. It warned 1500 IBM clients that the software they were using was illegal. SCO claimed that the Linux operating system sold by IBM included Unix code that was protected by copyright. In June 2003 the amount was increased to $3 billion and then to $5 billion. IBM reacted to the lawsuit with counter-claims against SCO. This, in turn, caught the attention of many companies that were using open source code such as Red Hat. On August 4, 2003 Red Hat started legal action against SCO claiming that some of the statements made by SCO indicated that anyone using a version of Linux that was not covered by a SCO UNIX license was violating copyright. Red Hat then created the Open Source Now Fund to financially support any legal expenses programmers and non-profit institutions that use the GPL might incur. On September 24, 2003, Hewlett-Packard (HP) also decided to create its own fund to guarantee continued use of its products to future users. Sun Microsystems guaranteed users of its products legal protection as well. On January 13, 2004, Novell followed suit. Novell's involvement was important because this company holds the copyright on Unix. The Unix system created by AT&T was sold to Novell, which then conceded some copyright to other companies, including SCO. Novell claims that there are no parts of the Unix code in Linux, and even if there were, since Novell holds the copyright, it would give its clients permission to use Linux. Novell's decision to side with Linux could lead other companies to do the same.

Following many warnings, on March 4, 2004, SCO filed lawsuits against two corporate users of Linux: AutoZone, the largest American retailer of automotive parts and accessories, and DaimlerChrysler, the automobile and truck manufacturer.

On July 19, 2004, Newsforge published a article reporting an HP memo that forecasts Microsoft waging a war on free software by using software patent infringements as its weapon. The memo stated: "Microsoft is going to use the legal system to shut down open-source software".[16] According to the article, Microsoft could attack not only Linux distributors but open source programmers as well. Microsoft has been spending an increasing amount of money on filing patents for even the most elemental computing components in its software products. Furthermore, Marshall Phelps, hired by Microsoft to help develop its intellectual property strategy, "...is on record as saying that Microsoft intends to spend $7bn annually on IP issues."

One proposal that has been made to help avoid these legal problems in the future is that from a certain moment on only code whose origin is verified by a certificate of origin will be included in the Linux kernel. The aim is to be able to more easily and precisely retrace the names of the authors of every single part of the code that makes up the heart of Linux. Using a Developer's Certificate of Origin (DCO), every developer has to "sign" every contribution he/she makes. In addition, developers have to certify one of the following three points:

- the contribution is either completely original,
- the contribution is based upon a previous work that is nonetheless covered under an open source license,
- the contribution comes from someone else who has certified one of the previous two points and has not been modified from its original form.

In another attempt to help avoid future legal actions by SCO or others, Pamela Jones, creator of pro-open source information site Groklaw.net, has started a project to clarify what the origins of Unix are. In her letter presenting the project on February 4, 2004, Jones states:

I want to do a systematic, comprehensive, and carefully documented history timeline relating to Unix and the Linux kernel, based, with his kind permission, on Eric Levenez's Unix History timeline chart, but from the perspective of tracing the code by copyright, patents, trade secret, and trademark. The idea is that the final timeline will be a publicly-available resource, released under a Creative Commons license, that will assist the community in defending against - or better yet in deterring - future lawsuits against GNU/Linux code.

On April 19, 2004 there was actually the first court ruling in favour of open source software. A three-judge panel in a Munich court ordered a preliminary injunction against the company Sitecom for violating GNU GPL. Sitecom was an open-source networking software distributed without attaching the GPL text and the source code. This ruling by a German court, which recognizes the legal validity of the GPL, could set a precedent in the history of this license. In the past, Microsoft has often questioned the legal validity GPL and, more recently, SCO has claimed that in its case against IBM it will show the weaknesses of this license. Although there are ambiguities in the license that will most likely be fought over, this case gives the community of GPL users hope for the future.

Open source software is particularly vulnerable to the sorts of attacks SCO has made. SCO, and anyone else for that matter, can see the source code of open source products such as Linux whereas the open source community does not have access to the code of proprietary software. This puts the open source community at a disadvantage. At the heart of all these legal cases is the issue of the relationships between intellectual property rights and software. To better understand these issues, in the next chapter we will discuss what intellectual property rights are and how they have been and are being applied to software.

Chapter 2

Software and Intellectual Property Rights

The evolution of the open source phenomenon, as we saw in the previous chapter, demonstrates that open source software is essentially different from proprietary software. But in what ways is it different? Could we say that open source software is the opposite or the antithesis of proprietary software?

We can only answer these questions if we look at the issue of Intellectual Property Rights (IPR) and software. Although IPR are applied to all products, the way they are applied in the case of software is different because software as a product is different. On the one hand, it is the result of human intellectual and creative efforts just like a book or other artistic expressions. In fact, just as copyright is applied to books and music, it is also applied to software. On the other hand, it is also a technological product with a sometimes significant economic value that induces those who have developed it or own it to protect it as much as possible. There is, in fact, much debate as to whether patents should applied to software the same way they are applied to other technological inventions. As we will see in this chapter, it is this very combination of characteristics that makes the issue of software and IPR complex. After defining software and describing its characteristics, we will focus on IPR in general, why they exist and what they protect. We will then analyze which types of IPR are most commonly used in the case of software. The last two parts of the chapter then deal with the issue of IPR and open source software in particular.

2.1 What is Software?

*S*oftware is a word many of us use without an in-depth understanding of what it means. One simple way to define software is to contrast it with hardware. In other words, software is the set of instructions executed by a computer whereas hardware is the physical device on which software runs. Another simple definition of software is that it is an application that performs a specific set of functions for the user, such as word processing.

These two basic definitions of software highlight a fundamental distinction between two types of software: system software and application software. In very basic terms, system software supports the execution of the application programs most users use, but it is not specific to any particular application. There are two types of system software: compilers and operating systems. A compiler is the software that reads the human-readable instructions written by the programmer and translates them into a computer-readable language in order to execute the instructions. A computer's operating system, e.g. Linux or Microsoft Windows, is the software that schedules tasks, allocates storage, handles the interface to peripheral hardware and presents a default interface to the user when no application program is running. Application programs are self-contained programs that perform a specific function directly for the user, e.g. spreadsheets and word processing.

To better understand how software actually works, it is helpful to think of three levels in the computing process: the instructions, the execution, the computing results. First the computer programmer writes the instructions. These human-readable instructions are what we call the source code. Since the source code cannot be read directly by a computer, a compiler translates it into the computer-readable code that is called object code. The computer's operating system then executes the instructions defined in the object code to produce the computing result.

One might ask why there are two types of code, i.e. source code that must be translated into the object code a computer can understand and execute. Wouldn't it simply be easier only to use object code? The answer has to do with the differences in complexity and sophistication between the human mind and computers. The object code is considered a low-level language because it consists almost entirely of ones and zeros or at most of a limited number of commands that have names rather than numbers. Though programmers could potentially use low-level code, writing programs that have to perform even the most basic data-processing operations would take a lot of time if written in object code. This is why high-level programming languages, such as "C", Fortran and Cobol, were developed: to help programmers write more complex instructions in less time.

At this point in our explanation we have to bring users into the picture. Most software users are only interested in computing results and are not the least bit interested in the code that leads to the computing result. However, some users are. Some users want access to the source code not only to read it, but to copy and modify it as well. This is why most commercial software is sold without the source code. By offering only object code, manufacturers are essentially denying software programmers the possibility to *see* the instructions that make the software do what it does. Furthermore, not only is source code human readable, but it also shows *how* the programmer arrived at the solution for the computing task at hand. Source code often contains comments through which programmers insert information into the computer program that does not become part of the object code. All of this information can be very valuable to other programmers because it may indicate which solutions were tried and failed, how certain problems were solved and even who was involved in programming the various parts of the code. In other words, the source code records the program's history. Without this information it is basically impossible to copy, reuse or even improve a program.

Basically, source code is the human accessible heart of any software program and that is why source code lies at the heart of the debate on software protection. In the following section, we will take a look at the evolution of intellectual property protection in general and then see how this directly applies to software.

2.2 Why Do Intellectual Property Rights Exist?

As has already been explained in Chapter 1, until software took on a commercial value the issue of protecting software did not even exist. Software was distributed and shared according to the same rules that govern the sharing of academic research. What changed? Why did property rights become an issue and in what way? To answer these questions, first we have to understand why and how software became a commercial good.

Every good is created and can then be used. From an economic point of view, these two moments correspond to production and consumption. The incentive for manufacturers to produce a good is to make up for production costs and make a profit by selling it. In the case of physical goods, it is to the benefit of the manufacturer to sell a limited number of physical goods at a relatively high price. On the contrary, it is to the benefit of the consumer to have a theoretically unlimited number of goods at a relatively low price. As far as consumption is concerned, we can say that goods have two main properties: rivalry and excludability. A good is rival when there is competition to use the same good, and when appropriation by one person reduces the quantity of the good available to other people. This concept applies where scarcity, in the economic sense, exists, as is the case with petrol. A good is excludable when others can be prevented from appropriating or consuming the good. A car is a good example: if I use my car others can't use it and so they are excluded.

Goods can be rival or non-rival and excludable or non-excludable. An important combination of these properties of goods is non-rivalry and non-excludability. If a good is non-rival and non-excludable, the number of people who can use it is theoretically unlimited and no one can impose limitations on its use, i.e. exclude others. A street sign is non-rival and non-excludable. A street sign gives information that is accessible to all regardless of how many people look at it. A street is non-excludable like the street sign, but rival like a car because the number of users at one given time is, in fact, limited. Though both the street and the street sign are public goods, the essence of the street sign is information while the street can be considered a physical good. This is an important distinction because whereas information is non-rival and non-excludable, physical goods are rival, even if not always excludable, as is the case of our street.

How do these considerations apply to software products? Software is an information product. Theoretically information is non-rival and non-excludable because many people can use it at the same time and no one can be excluded from the information itself. Therefore, considering software to be exclusively an information product would benefit the consumer, but not the manufacturer. What costs the manufacturer the most is the development process that leads to the creation of the first copy of a software product, whereas the cost of reproducing the same software product is marginal. If there are no limitations on copying, anybody can copy and distribute software at a price that is equal to the trivial cost of reproduction. In this case, the incentive to produce the good has been lost because the manufacturer has not made up for the production costs. The solution then, from a production point of view, is to protect the information contained in software products using intellectual property rights.

When software began to be a commercial good in the late 1970s and early 1980s, companies had to find a way to make software a rival and excludable good. To do this, companies turned to Intellectual Property Rights (IPR) to limit the terms of use of their software. Intellectual property rights grant authors, or in this case software companies, the possibility to control the copying, modification and distribution of their own products. This control makes software excludable inasmuch as the company can allow or prohibit access to the product. In this way, companies can distribute software at a price that is much higher than the cost of reproduction. By being able to make a profit from selling software, companies can justify the cost of developing software.

What steps did companies first take to use intellectual property rights to protect their software? And in what different ways can software be considered intellectual property? We will now consider the four different ways of protecting intellectual property and how each applies to software.

2.3 Types of IPR and How They are Applied to Software

The four types of intellectual property rights generally used are: trade secret, trademark, copyright, and patent. Most of the original laws regarding intellectual property rights were first written before software became a commercial product. Therefore, first we will give a general definition of each type of IPR and then consider how each has been applied or is being applied to software.

A **trade secret** is confidential information, including a practice, formula, method, process, program, device or technique, that a company uses to compete with other businesses for its own economic benefit. In order for this information to be considered a trade secret, considerable efforts must be made to maintain its secrecy. A classic example of trade secret is the recipe to Coca-Cola. "Having a trade secret means that you have a legal cause of action for damages, or an injunction to stop the use, if another party steals, copies or uses your trade secret without your permission."[17] However, a trade secret is not registered and cannot, therefore, benefit from the protection offered by other forms of IPR, i.e. copyright and patent. In order to register a product or process, at least some information regarding it must be disclosed, thus infringing the trade secret.

In the early days of computer science technologies, software was distributed freely without any limitations and was considered, as was scientific research, to be a public good. However, as we have already seen, there is no profit in selling a public good and small profits could not justify investing large amounts of money in software development. Trade secret laws worked well in the early days of computing technology because the standardized programming languages that are used today had still not been developed. The use of low-level languages required highly specialized skills that only a limited number of people had. In this scenario, it was relatively easy to keep software "secrets" within an organization. Even when software began to be distributed on a more commercial level, e.g. MS/DOS software in the early 1980s, it was done so under tight contractual control, again making it easy to control trade secret.

A **trademark** is a word, name, symbol or device used by a business to distinguish itself and its goods from others. The purpose of a trademark is not to prevent others from making the same goods or selling them, but rather to prevent others from using the same symbol, word or device. In theory, this should prevent the public from being deceived about the origin and quality of a product.

In the case of software, well-known examples of trademark are Microsoft Windows and Microsoft Office. One of the most successful open source software projects, the Linux operating system, has high brand recognition for the trademarked name "Linux" which is often accompanied by the penguin logo Tux.

Copyright protects published or unpublished literary, scientific and artistic works, such as books, software and music, that have been fixed in a tangible or material form. Copyright laws grant the author the exclusive right to copy, sell, license, distribute, modify, translate and, in general, do whatever he/she wants to with the original work. Copyright laws were created to encourage authorship by protecting copying. Though each country has its own specific copyright laws, almost all major nations follow the Berne copyright convention, which states that almost all things are copyrighted by default the moment they are written. However, in order to sue for damages, a copyright must be registered. While copyright protects the form of the work, i.e. you cannot copy it, and the overall content in the work, i.e. you cannot create derivative works based on the same set of ideas as the original, it does not prohibit anyone from creating new works by developing ideas from the original work.

As we have already said, trade secret was effective in protecting proprietary software until programming languages and operating systems became more standardized in the 1980s. With standardization came an increased possibility for programmers to understand the source code of any given software program. In other words, the secret inherent in source code could no longer be protected simply by trade secret. A more effective method of protecting source was needed so companies and lawmakers turned to copyright.

From a legal point of view, copyright is a contract made between an author and a user that stipulates what the user can or cannot do with the author's work. In the context of the mass distribution of software, it was impossible for every author to stipulate this sort of contract with every user. Therefore, laws had to be made to define general norms that determined how software could be distributed and reproduced. Software copyright laws generally allow the user the sole privilege of using the software while the author keeps every other right for the commercial use of the software for him/herself.

In the early 1980s the United States (1980), Australia (1981), Great Britain, France and Germany (1985) began to make specific copyright laws for software. In 1991, the European Community issued a council directive (91/250/EEC) on the protection of computer programs that states: "...Member States shall protect computer programs, by copyright, as literary works within the meaning of the Berne Convention for the Protection of Literary and Artistic Works". In fact, the idea that source code could be considered original expression, i.e. a sort of literary work, became accepted as programming languages began to resemble human languages.

At this point the problem of deciding what could or could not be protected by copyright became a matter of discussion. Since software can be copied not only by copying the source code, but by copying the object code as well, both codes are protected by copyright. The power of copyright to protect software is taken to extremes in the "RAM copy" doctrine. According to this doctrine, even just running a computer program without permission or authorization can be considered an infringement of copyright law since to do so the object code of a computer program has to be copied from the hard drive into the memory of a computer.

A **patent** gives the creator of a process or product the exclusive right, also called monopoly right, of the use, manufacture and sale of the invention or products deriving from the invention. It is important to clarify that a patent does not grant the right to make, use, sell or import the product or process, but rather the right to exclude others from making, using, selling or importing it.

Patent legislation was created to protect original inventions and the investments incurred to make the discovery. This was considered to be a way to stimulate the development and progress of science and technology. To patent an invention it must be original and offer a significant advancement in knowledge. "When a patent is granted to an inventor, it becomes a public document that fully discloses the details of the invention so that others skilled in the technology can duplicate the results achieved by the patented invention; however, the invention owner retains the sole right to exclude others from making, selling, using, or importing the invention."[18] Patents currently last for 20 years. The owner has a legal monopoly on the invention for that time period and when it is up the knowledge becomes part of the public domain. The right to exclude others from using the invention is what has made patents very effective in many industrial fields, especially from a commercial point of view.

At the European Patent Convention in Monaco in 1973, lawmakers decided that "European patents shall be granted for any inventions which are susceptible of industrial application, which are new and which involve an inventive step."[19] Mathematical methods, business models and computer programs were explicitly excluded from this definition of patentable inventions as they were considered to be ideas and not inventions or applications.

In 1995, after years of unclear decisions regarding software and patents in the United States, the USPTO (United States Patent and Trademark Office) adopted its *Final Computer Related Examination Guidelines* which effectively made it legal to patent software. Business methods, such as Amazon.com's "1-click shopping", were considered to be patentable as well. Following this decision, the situation regarding the patentability of software began to change in Europe as well. There are currently 30,000 European software patents, 75% of which are owned by large non-European companies. In September 2003, the European Parliament approved a draft Directive on the Patentability of Computer-Implemented Inventions which limited the use of software patents in Europe. However, following opposition to the draft, in May 2004 the Council of the EU proposed a new text which widens the scope of software patentability in Europe.

The changes from the decisions made in the early 1970s against patenting software to the situation today, in which hundreds of thousands of software patents have been issued, closely follows the evolution of the software industry. As the industry grew, so did the desire to protect its intellectual property. Whereas copyright has generally been considered an acceptable way of protecting software, the issue of patenting software is quite controversial.

First, we must clarify that a software patent is actually a process patent. According to the USPTO's guidelines, an idea cannot be patented but a process that leads to a real-world result can. In the case of software, the main ideas behind the software are the algorithms. The algorithms are considered processes that lead to computing results. This said, the main arguments in support of patenting software are those used to justify any type of patent. One of the arguments deals with the concept of protecting the inventor. An inventor has the right to be protected when the development of an invention requires high investment costs. A patent can be justified insomuch as it allows the inventor to make up for his/her investments. Another argument in support of patents is that they offer a trade-off: the inventor can financially exploit the patent for a set number of years in exchange for depositing the inventive knowledge.

There are also several arguments against patenting software. First of all, although software has functional characteristics similar to those of more traditional products, and therefore can be considered patentable, it lacks the physical aspect. Many argue that algorithms cannot be considered patentable processes but, like mathematical models, must be considered ideas and as such part of the public domain. According to the law in most countries, abstract ideas cannot be patented. When a programmer develops an idea (an algorithm) and creates a product with it (the software product), the inventor and product are protected by copyright laws. Though copyright prohibits the copy and use of software without the consent of the owner of the copyright, it does not prohibit software programmers from using the algorithms and techniques developed by others to create new software that can carry out different functions. In other words, what is protected is the final product, the software that has been developed, and not the abstract ideas or algorithms contained in it. For example, copyright can protect a specific software for compressing data but not the idea of compressing data or one of the algorithms used to compress data in that software. On the other hand, a patent on the algorithm used to compress the data would actually exclude others from even using the same algorithm in different, improved or more innovative software, or at least exclude those unable or unwilling to pay to use the license.

Secondly, in the case of software patents there is no guarantee that the inventive knowledge behind the invention be deposited. This is because the real contents of the knowledge can be found in the source code and depositing patents does not require inventors to reveal the source code. In this way, one can have a patent and at the same time keep some parts of the product, i.e. the source code, secret. It is also interesting to note that most of the software patents that have already been granted do not contain information that is a significant advancement for knowledge.[20] What's more, the patent process is slow and long and often the knowledge that was to be protected by the patent is obsolete by the time the patent is actually granted.

Thirdly, in traditional industries the 20-year duration of a patent is accepted as long enough to give the owner an economic advantage but not too long to slow down innovation. This is not the case when we consider software. Since the life cycle of software is significantly shorter than that of more traditional products, patents could limit innovation in this field.

Another way to evaluate the positive and negative aspects of patenting software is to consider who has used this form of intellectual property protection. Most software patents are owned by large companies that can afford the very high costs involved. These companies can afford to deal with the costs of eventual software infringement or set up cross-licensing agreements with other large companies. Many software patents have been used with the sole aim of preventing others from using the same ideas and/or entering the market. These patents may not, therefore, correspond to an actual invention, but rather might simply be a way of obtaining a competitive advantage.[21]

Patenting software can also be a strong deterrent to Small and Medium Enterprises (SMEs) and individual programmers. SMEs do not usually have the financial resources to take part in patent competition. The effect is to concentrate knowledge in a limited fraction of the industry and, again, to limit innovation. On an individual level, even if a programmer writes his/her own software from scratch, he/she could unwittingly infringe existing software patents. Consequently, programmers might be discouraged from working on development projects that might lead to legal battles with a possible patent owner. When uncertain, programmers prefer to avoid projects that could have legal risks. This has the effect of limiting the innovative potential connected to a certain product or application. Software patents could, therefore, distance many programmers who are already a part of the development community from innovative projects.

A practical example of how software patents can create problems is that of the LZW algorithm (after its inventors Lempel-Ziv-Welch). Among its many applications, this algorithm is used to compress GIF images (Graphics Interchange Format), one of the most common formats used to exchange images. A patent was filed for the LZW algorithm in 1983, but when one of the authors, Welch, presented the algorithm in IEEE's magazine *Computer* in 1984, no mention was made of the patent. Since Welch described the algorithm very clearly and it was a simple procedure, it soon became a commonly used technique for data compression, not only for GIF. A CompuServe Associate designed GIF without being aware that there was a patent on the LZW algorithm. In 1987, CompuServe released GIF as a free and open format and it soon became a worldwide standard. For several years Unisys, the company that held the LZW algorithm patent, did not require anyone using the algorithm to pay for a license. This changed when it became a standard with GIF and was widely used. Following much controversy, Unisys announced that developers of certain categories of software would have to pay a licensing fee. Today, the GIF format has been surpassed by other free formats and the US (2003) and European and Japanese patents (2004) have expired. Nonetheless, the example clearly demonstrates the confusion and limitations software patents can impose on the development of new software.[22]

2.4 Categories of Software

In order to understand better how intellectual property rights are actually applied to software products, it is important to understand that there are different categories of software. We can divide software into various categories depending on three characteristics in particular: cost, source code distribution and rules governing use. On one end of the spectrum we have public domain software which is free of charge and has no rules governing its use. On the other end, we have proprietary software which is often expensive, does not come with the source code and whose use is protected by copyright or patent laws. In between these two extremes we can find free/open source software, freeware and shareware (see Table 2.1).

Table 2.1 – Comparison of categories of software.

	Public Domain software	Free/open source software	Freeware software	Shareware software	Proprietary software
Example	HTML	GNU Linux	Acrobat Reader	Apogee software	Microsoft Windows
Free of charge	Yes	Yes	Yes	Limited	No
Unconditional use	Yes	Yes	No	No	No
Source code open	Not always	Yes	No	No	No
Freedom to modify	Yes	Yes	No	No	No
Protection of freedom	No	Yes	No	No	No

Public domain software

In the case of public domain software, the author or owner of the software has given up all his/her intellectual property rights. Public domain software is considered part of the public's cultural heritage and thus anyone can use and build upon it without restriction. There is no copyright protecting public domain software. The absence of rights means that anyone could potentially request ownership of copies or modified versions of public domain software, changing the status of the software. Well-known examples of public domain software are programming languages such as HTML and the internet protocol TCP/IP.

Free/open source software

Software can be considered free or open source software if it guarantees free-of-charge access to the source code that generates it. Free/open source software is different from public domain software in that it is protected by copyright and specific open source licenses. With open source licenses, specific permission does not have to be granted by the author in order to use, diffuse and/or modify this type of software. Though the name of the author of one of these products must often be included in copies and derivative works, no one person or group can claim to be the owner of free/open source software.

This type of software has been called free not so much for the fact that it is free of charge but for the freedoms it guarantees:

- freedom to use the software for any purpose;
- freedom to study source codes and use them for one's own needs;
- freedom to distribute copies of the original software;
- freedom to improve the program and publicly distribute derivative works so that everyone can benefit from the improvements.

Examples of free/open source software are the Linux operating system and the Apache web server.

Freeware

Freeware is software that can be freely distributed, free of charge, even for private use but without a profit being made on it. For example, commercial companies cannot use freeware. The difference between freeware and free/open source software is that freeware does not come with the source code. In other words, it respects the ideal of free of charge and some of the freedoms guaranteed by free software, but not the freedom of source code availability. Therefore, though it may be difficult without the source code, freeware can not only be used, but copied, modified and distributed so long as it is for personal, non-profit use.

Adobe Acrobat Reader and CutePDF Writer, a free version of the commercial PDF creation software, are well-known examples of freeware.

Shareware

Shareware is software that is distributed free of charge, often via free download from the Internet in order to bypass retailers and go directly to the end-user. However, users must pay fees either to use the product for a prolonged period of time or to access expanded features, services or new versions of the product. Shareware is often used by companies to launch a product; initial versions of the product are shareware and then later versions are proprietary. A rather well-known example of shareware is Apogee software. Apogee is a video game publisher that would sell the first installment of a game trilogy for free (usually via download from the Internet) and then sell the remaining installments for a fee (by post).

Proprietary software

Proprietary software is protected by licenses that control the use, modification and distribution of the software. They are sold at an often high cost and do not give access to the source code. Almost all of the freedoms guaranteed in the definition of free software, e.g. to copy, distribute and modify the software, are denied in the case of proprietary software; the explicit permission of the owner of the property rights must be given in order to access these freedoms. Basically, the only freedom users of this type of software are granted is the freedom to use the product. Probably the most famous examples of proprietary software are Microsoft Windows and Office.

To complete this brief overview of software categories, we must highlight two distinctions: the difference between the commercial and proprietary aspects of software and the difference between the Free Software Foundation (FSF) and the Open Source Initiative (OSI).

Proprietary software is commercial in the sense that it is developed with the aim of making a profit on licensing fees. However, a profit can also be generated using alternative means, i.e. not through licensing fees. For example, several business created around open source software products make a profit by selling packaging, service, etc. for the open source software products. We will take a more in-depth look at these new business models in Chapter 6.

One fundamental difference between the FSF and the OSI is that the former has often been wary of the interest and participation of companies whereas the latter has maintained that professionals and companies must be involved. The main aim of the FSF is to recreate an environment where software is completely free. Most of the attention is focused on the GNU (GNU's not Unix) project, whose goal is to develop a complete operating system that can substitute commercial versions. The FSF considers software to be knowledge, i.e. a public good, and defends the fact that it should be free. The restrictions imposed on software by intellectual property rights are considered completely unacceptable. However, this position tends to de-motivate the participation of the IT industry thus isolating the FSF from an important part of the development community. On the other hand, one of the main goals of the OSI is to set up collaborative projects in order to take advantage of the professional skills available in companies and develop higher quality products. Some projects, such as Apache and Mozilla, were started up by, and continue to be developed in collaboration with, commercial companies and professionals.

A second difference is that while the motivations behind the FSF are prevalently ideological, the ones behind the OSI are more technical. The OSI organizes and manages collaborative projects between companies and the independent community of volunteer developers with the aim of creating development processes that are more economical and able to produce improved software and standards. By doing this, the OSI hopes to stimulate the market and innovation by opposing monopolies and thus favouring competition. Open source software is an attempt to reach a compromise between the financial goals of companies and the freedom and openness of open source software, a compromise the FSF is not willing to make.

2.5 Copyright and Open Source Software Licenses

So far in this chapter we have seen how intellectual property rights apply to software and what different types of software there are. Now we are going to take a more in-depth look at the relationship between open source software and intellectual property rights. Copyright is the form of IPR that the open source community has exploited the most.

We could say that the open source community has made a different interpretation of what copyright should guarantee in order to benefit not only the author/creator or innovative and original works but progress and society as a whole. From the moment a computer programmer writes the instructions that make up the source code of a program, it contains copyrightable material and is thus protected. Open source licenses take this protection and add additional protection to guarantee users have free access to the source code and the possibility to modify it. Richard Stallman, founder of the free software movement, has stated, "Proprietary software developers use copyright to take away the users' freedom; we use copyright to guarantee their freedom".[23]

To understand better how the open source community uses copyright protection, we can compare open source products to a commons. A commons is an area everyone and anyone has access to and where people can do what they want to, within certain limits. In order to avoid anarchy and chaos and guarantee that the commons is a pleasant place to go, certain rules must be followed. These rules basically deal with mutual respect: don't do in the commons what you wouldn't want others to do. The open source community more or less functions the same way. The founding principle of the movement was not to oppose commercial software, but rather to oppose the limitations placed on what could or could not be done with commercial software. The commons had been closed off to the public and the open source community decided to re-open it and lay down some new rules for those who would use it.

Proprietary software closes the commons by allowing users the sole right to use a software product, but not to modify, distribute or copy it. Furthermore, users have to pay to use proprietary software. Open source software opens up the commons by giving users the source code free of charge and allowing them to modify, distribute and copy it. However, if open source software was not protected in any way, it would be part of the public domain and as such a third party could appropriate it and transform it into proprietary software. For example, HTML (Hypertext Markup Language) is public domain software and has been the subject of appropriation by those who wish to have greater control over it. Microsoft and Netscape have both developed, promoted and protected different versions of HTML. This has created barriers to the possibility of HTML becoming the one shared standard for the publication of information on the Internet.

So how does the open source community use copyright to protect freedom and openness? By turning the concept of copyright upside down. The Free Software Foundation created the phrase "copyleft – all rights reversed", playing on the phrase "copyright – all rights reserved", and turned the copyright symbol © upside down ☺. As Stallman describes: "To copyleft a program, we first state that it is copyrighted; then we add distribution terms, which legally give everyone the rights to use, modify, and redistribute the program's code *or any program derived from it* but only if the distribution terms are unchanged. Thus, the code and the freedoms become legally inseparable".[24] For example, the GNU/Linux operating system uses a copyleft license, the GNU General Public License (GPL), which states that any derivative work must maintain the same terms as the original GPL license.[25] The GPL and all the other copyleft licenses are based on the concept of share and share alike.

Nonetheless, not all open source software is protected by copyleft. Non-copyleft software does not impose the "share alike" restriction. In other words, software derived from a non-copyleft product does not have to use the same license as the original. Another famous open source product, the Apache web server software, is an example of a non-copyleft product. The Apache license allows any user to build his/her own version of the product starting from the original product, and to then distribute it according to the terms he/she feels are most advantageous. In other words, there is nothing to prohibit the derivative work of a non-copyleft product from being distributed as a proprietary product. However, the derivative work must clearly identify in exact terms its origins, i.e. the non-copyleft product, and, more importantly, should it become proprietary, it cannot use the same name as the original product. In the case of Apache, if a derived version became proprietary, it would have to clearly state it was a derivative work of Apache and it could not be called Apache.

Figure 2.1 shows how copyright can be applied to software. The type of protection depends on the rights and limitations the software license imposes on the user. As can be seen in the figure, the question "Is the source code open?" is an issue only if there is an affirmative answer to the question "Is there copyright?". This means that open source software falls into the category of software protected by some form of copyright. The figure also highlights how the degree of freedom of access to a product decreases significantly as we move from left (public domain software) to right (proprietary software). Similarly, as we move from left

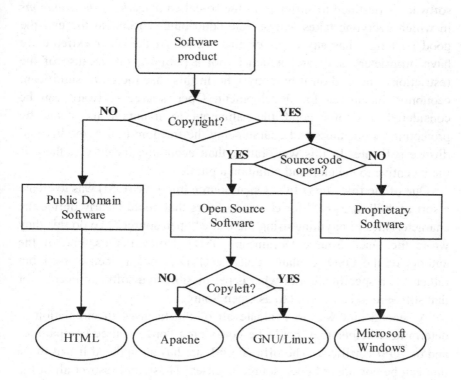

Figure 2.1 – How copyright can be applied to software (adapted from Lessig, 2002).

to right, the characteristics of software as a public good decrease and the possibilities of making a profit from selling software increase.

On the left-hand side of the figure, in the public domain, the problem of incentives for development, i.e. provision, is more relevant. Vice versa, on the right-hand side, in the case of proprietary software, the problem of consumption of software as a public good, i.e. diffusion, is more critical. Based on these considerations, companies can choose which type of intellectual property protection they want to adopt. Their choice can be to promote diffusion, which will increase with consumption (*demand side* strategy) or maximize profits by controlling the number of goods distributed (*supply side* strategy).

If we go back to the issue of software as a public good, we can see that when software is part of the public domain it is a public good, but in this case there aren't any incentives for development. Public domain software is destined to suffer from the so-called *tragedy of the commons* in which everyone takes and no one contributes so that in the end the good no longer has any of its original value. At the other extreme we have proprietary software, which is not a public good because of the restrictions imposed on it by copyright. In this case there *are* significant economic incentives for development. Open source software can be considered a public good that attempts to maintain its status by protecting its openness and guaranteeing the freedom to use, modify and diffuse software. In this way, rather than economic incentives, there is the incentive to develop and maintain a public good.

One of the first aims of the Open Source Initiative (OSI) was to create a sort of "bill of rights" for computer users that could clearly define the characteristics of anything using the name "open source". To do this they wrote the Open Source Definition (OSD). Bruce Perens, one of the authors of the OSD, explains that the OSD is not a license itself but rather "... a specification of what is permissible in a software license for that software to be referred to as Open Source".[26]

A second aim was to evaluate all of the licenses in circulation to determine whether they could be considered "open source compatible" and/or "OSI certified". The official OSI site has an updated list of those that can be considered open source licenses. Those that respect all of the criteria in the OSD can be accompanied by the official statement: "This software is OSI Certified Open Source Software. OSI Certified is a certification mark of the Open Source Initiative".

All open source licenses must respect the founding principles laid down in the Open Source Definition, among which are free distribution, availability of source code, possibility to create derivative works, integrity of the author's source code and no discrimination against persons, groups or fields. There are, however, significant differences between the different licenses which depend on the following criteria:

- the possibility to link the product to or distribute it with other open source products that have different licenses;
- the possibility to link the product to or distribute it with both open source and proprietary products;
- the degree of protection of the freedom rights, i.e. the rights to use, copy, modify and distribute the product.

In order to better understand these differences, it might be useful to compare four of the most well-known open source licenses: the GNU General Public License (GPL), the GNU Library or "Lesser" General Public License (LGPL), the Mozilla Public License (MPL), and the Berkeley Software Distribution license (BSD).

General Public License (GPL)

The General Public License was created by the Free Software Foundation for the GNU project. It is one of the most restrictive open source licenses. It guarantees the freedom to use, modify and distribute products. In fact, it was designed to ensure the free distribution of copies, access to the source codes and the possibility to modify them and reuse parts to create new free software. The source code must always be available to or easy to obtain by anyone who wants it. It is restrictive in that the source code of a product protected by the GPL cannot be linked to other source codes that are not covered by the GPL and any derivative works must also be covered by the GPL. In other words, once a product has a GPL it will always have the GPL and any derivative work will as well. These characteristics have led the GPL to be defined a "viral" license. Defenders of the GPL consider this to be positive since it grants the same freedoms and permissions to everyone. However, some businesses consider it to be a negative aspect of the GPL: the GPL is a virus that can only transmit GPL to other works. In other words, the GPL completely separates the free software community from commercial/ proprietary companies.

Lesser General Public License (LGPL)

Libraries are routines that can be used by executable programs but are not part of the programs themselves. Therefore, a proprietary library can be used together with free software just as proprietary software can use a library developed by the open source community. For this reason, the FSF created the Library General Public License (LGPL) specifically for libraries. The LGPL differs from the GPL in that it allows proprietary software to use open source libraries without having to change the terms of the proprietary license. Since it is a version of the GPL with fewer restrictions, the first "L" in the name came to mean, and was eventually changed to, "Lesser" rather than "Library".

Mozilla Public License (MPL)

The Mozilla Public License is a creation of Netscape. The first open license created by Netscape, the Netscape Public License (NPL) retained certain privileges for the company, such as the possibility to keep some parts of the product developed in collaboration with the open source community closed. The community did not accept the NPL so Netscape quickly developed the MPL. The Mozilla Public License is a copyleft license even if it gives permission to integrate software covered by the MPL with other commercial products.

Berkeley Software Distribution License (BSD License)

The Berkeley Software Distribution license originally covered the version of Unix developed by Berkeley University during the 1970s. When AT&T decided to commercialize Unix at the end of the 1980s, the new proprietary operating system contained both BSD code and proprietary code. The original programmers of BSD Unix decided to separate the BSD code from the proprietary code and began to distribute it under the BSD license. The license required that recognition be given to those who held the copyright, i.e. the University of Berkeley. Over time the name of other organizations that had supported the development of this software were added. In 1999, Berkeley University decided to eliminate the recognition clause from the official version of the BSD license.

Although the BSD license satisfies the Open Source Definition, it gives permission to keep modifications to the original code private. In other words, anyone who modifies the original software is not required to distribute the new code or apply the same license to the product the new code has been generated from. In fact, the Open Source Definition does not require derived versions of an open source product to be covered by the same license as the original product. The BSD license gives greater freedom to adapt and mix code covered by the BSD license with other codes. This does mean, however, that programmers can refuse to release the modifications they have made to the community and this can impede some opportunities for collaboration. This might be the reason that the BSD is not as diffused as the GPL.

2.6 Open Source Software and Patents

We have seen how the open source community has been able to take advantage of copyright and develop licenses that protect the freedoms the OSI wants to guarantee. On the contrary, patents are proving to be a problem for open source software. The fact that the source code of all open source products is open and available, exposes these products to more risk of patent lawsuits. In other words, the proof needed to show infringement of a patent could easily be found in the source code of an open source product. For example, an open source project could potentially independently develop an algorithm that has already been patented, but have no knowledge of the patent. If this algorithm is then included in an open source product, anyone who uses the product containing the algorithm that is covered by patent is infringing the law. These users could, therefore, be prohibited from running the software. Theoretically, third parties could strategically obtain patents to put open source products at a competitive disadvantage. This type of patent has actually come to be known as an "open-source-blocking patent".

The evolution of the open source phenomenon is influenced by decisions that regard patent laws. The proposal to allow software patents in Europe will certainly have significant effects on the evolution, or better involution, of the open source phenomenon. The actual benefits that such a law might have must be thoroughly analyzed. What added value could patenting software offer the industry and in particular SMEs? Furthermore, what additional protection is actually offered to inventors by applying patent law rather than just copyright law? And, finally, might the present situation, i.e. the fact that software cannot be patented in Europe, actually be a competitive advantage that could favour the European information technology industry?[27]

The fact that the number of applications for software process patents has grown significantly in the past few years indicates that this trend is taking hold and is a real risk for the open source community. Not only do these patents threaten specific open source projects, but they "may generally impede the growth of the open source approach by taking up *algorithm space*."[28] Though there are numerous algorithms to be used in source code, the number is not infinite. Therefore, as more and more patents are made for algorithms, the flexibility programmers have at their disposal decreases.

At the beginning of the chapter we posed the question: "Could we say that open source software is the opposite or the antithesis of proprietary software?". It should now be clear that the answer to this question is no. Open source software is not the opposite of proprietary software because, like proprietary software, it uses IPR. For example, both the "GNU" and "Linux" names and their logos, a gnu and a penguin named "Tux", demonstrate that the free/open source communities use trademarks to distinguish their products from others. However, it should also be clear how open source software is different from proprietary software. For example, rather than using copyright to protect source code, the open source community exploits it to guarantee the freedom to use, modify and distribute its software. Another fundamental difference between these two types of software is the fact that open source software is developed by a community of volunteer developers. Who are these developers? Why do they dedicate their free time to voluntarily contribute to developing open source software? How are they organized? While this chapter has discussed how open source *software* is unique, the next chapter focuses on how the open source *community* is unique.

Chapter 3

The Organization of the
Open Source Community

In 1976, when he was 21, in "Open Letter to Hobbyists" Bill Gates wrote: "Who can afford to do professional work for nothing? What hobbyist can put their three man-years into programming, finding all bugs, documenting his product, and distribute for free?"[29] In this letter he claimed that the ethic of free-of-charge software was wrong and that there was a commercial market for software. He was right that there was a market for software, but 24 years later a young university student in Finland disagreed that the ethic of free software was wrong. In an on-line message, Linus Torvalds, then 22, publicized his creation LINUX by writing an online message in which he stated: "This is a program for hackers by a hacker. I've enjoyed doing it, and somebody might enjoy looking at it and even modifying it for their own needs."[30] The result was the creation of an international community of hackers who voluntarily dedicate their free time to developing open source software. Hackers are people whose hobby and passion is figuring out computer problems. They should not be confused with crackers, who are people that use their computer skills to commit illegitimate and/or illegal actions, i.e. break computer security systems, create viruses, etc. Since Torvald's first message the community has grown exponentially and produced many high quality, technologically advanced products.

How is this possible? How does this community work? This chapter deals with the open source community. First we will identify the key players in the community and describe the relationships existing between them. Then we will take a look at the demographics of the software developers in particular. We will also consider what motivates individuals, organizations and society to keep the community alive and functioning. After having considered "who" the community is, we will focus on "how" the community works. We will do this through an analysis of the main characteristics of the organization of the open source community, (open participation and bottom-up organization) and of the open source software development process (fast development and parallel development).

3.1 "Who" is the Open Source Community?

Open source products are developed within a community made up of a heterogeneous group of independent players who interact but are driven by different interests and motivations. [31] This community, though seemingly chaotic, actually has specific organizational characteristics.

Some authors refer to the open source community using the metaphor of a bazaar since it expresses the idea of the frenzy and chaos with which the activities in the community are carried out. [32] The open source community has also been seen as an immense "magic cauldron" of ideas to which volunteers contribute on a continuous basis. [33] Anyone can draw from this cauldron to suit his/her needs without having to contribute money or knowledge.

The community of players meets online and creates a dynamic virtual team, i.e. a team characterized by the constant coming and going of players who contact each other via virtual meetings such as forums and mailing lists. These meeting points make it possible to diffuse concepts, ideas and strategies to the whole community without dispersing or slowing down the flow of information and decisions. What is interesting about this community is that this virtual team is made up not only of software developers, but of other players as well.

By observing numerous open source projects, it is possible to identify five categories of players involved in the community: users, prosumers, leader teams, companies and non-commercial/public institutions. These five categories and the relationships that exist between them are shown in Figure 3.1.

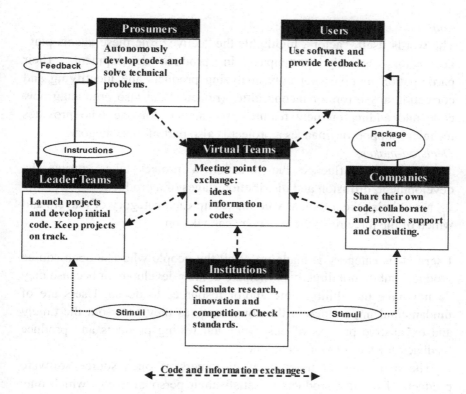

Figure 3.1 – Structure of the open source community.

Depending on what they do, players can take on one or more of the following three roles: customer, actor or decision-maker. [34] Before describing each category and the various roles that players can take on, let's look at a brief definition of each role.

Customers
Customers neither take part in the community nor finance product development. Their relationship with the open source community is limited to using open source products and exploiting the community to meet their own needs.

Actors
The words itself, "actor", highlights the "active" role these agents play, i.e. actors actively participate in product development. Their participation involves not only analyzing products and identifying and correcting any errors or incongruities (re-actor) but also producing new code and adding on new features (pro-actor). Anyone who provides technical support or finances a project is also part of this category.

Decision-makers
These players influence the direction a project takes during the development, diffusion and distribution stages of a product.

Now, let's take a look at who makes up each category of players and which of the three roles these players can take on.

Users. This category is made up of all the people who use open source products but do not directly participate in their development because they do not have the ability, time and/or resources to do so. Users are of fundamental importance to the community as they carry out the timely and exhaustive process of observing and testing products and produce feedback for the software developers.

The main role of users is as customers of open source software products. They use products to satisfy their personal needs, which may be both professional and personal in nature. Users are also often defined using the term "free riders" since they use the fruit of the community's work without directly contributing to development. Nonetheless, the presence of free riding is not looked down upon within the community because free riders *are* actually indirectly involved in product development. The feedback users provide is considered to be a significant and integral part of the development process. Feedback can contain both criticism of existing features and ideas for new ones. Furthermore, since users use the software in real situations, they can assess the overall quality of the products. This assessment implicitly leads to product selection and thus influences the evolution of open source software products. This is why we can say that users can have some of the characteristics of actors and decision-makers in the development process.

Prosumers. Prosumers (**pro**ducer and con**sumer**) are software developers who actively participate in product development to meet their own needs, for the pure pleasure of developing products, and, in many cases, with the hope of improving their own professional prospects. This group is the nucleus of open source software development. It is generally made up of people who come from different walks of life and use their free time to work on the development of a code. These people might be students or software developers/ professionals with very different cultural backgrounds and professional needs.

The main role of prosumers is as actors. The voluntary work of these agents provides the main contributions to product development. The role of actor can have two different connotations. In the first case, reaction, the agent's responsibility is to correct errors and imperfections in the code (*re-actor*). In this case, prosumers help stabilize products so that they can actually be used by customers. The second behavior is related to production. In this case, prosumers are involved in the research and implementation of new features and consequently contribute to the creation of new code (*pro-actor*). Nonetheless, the word itself "prosumer", made by putting the words producer and consumer together, shows the twofold nature of these agents. In fact, in addition to being actors in the development of codes, they are often the first ones to use open source products, i.e. customers. Finally, prosumers can make proposals and thus influence the direction the development of a product goes in. In other words, they have a significant role in the management of development processes as well and are, in this sense, decision-makers.

Leader Teams. This category is made up of software developers and is a sort of elite group chosen by the community based on merit. This group of people is given the authority and responsibility of managing projects. A leader team is made up of a tight circle of prosumers who have participated in the definition and development of open source products from the beginning of the projects.

The main role of the leader teams is as decision-makers. Leaders dedicate much of their time to planning, managing and checking the product development processes and often do not participate in programming. They guide the development process of a project and are responsible for project management. The leader teams have to try and resolve any disputes regarding the project. They are responsible for motivating development efforts and integrating the various contributions received. Finally, since the leaders are made up of prosumers, they continue to carry out the role of actor and customer, even if to a lesser degree.

Companies. This category is made up of the companies that are interested in the open source community and its products. They interact with the open source community by using open source software, financing product development, and/or participating in the development of software. Therefore, they can either influence the development process and evolution of products or simply support the community.

Companies can have one or more of the three roles. Many companies have chosen to use open source products for their own production and management processes and have thus helped diffuse these products. By using these products, they act as customers, and by diffusing them they act as decision-makers. Other companies get more involved by having their personnel directly participate in the development of open source software. In this case, they have a role as actors in the community. The different ways companies can and are interacting with the open source community are dealt with in Chapter 6.

Institutions. This category of players is essentially made up of universities and governments. Some universities have created the cultural environment in which many open source products have been developed. Some important products, such as Linux, were created thanks to the technical support, and sometimes financial support, of universities. Recently, governments have also shown interest in open source products first by carrying out studies and then, sometimes, by promoting the use of open source software in their own structures.

Universities can take on all three roles. They are among the main users of open source products and as such are customers. Many professors and students are also involved in researching and developing open standards and open source products, and are, therefore, actors.

Finally, some universities are even decision-makers in that they support the community and products through specific investments.

So far, governments have mostly taken on the role of customers, though they could potentially play an important role as decision-makers as well. As we will see in Chapter 7, many governments are considering adopting OSS or have already started doing so. If they actually do start implementing OSS on a large scale, this decision could influence the software choices the public makes.

Table 3.1 sums up the different characteristics taken on by agents depending on the role they play. [35]

Table 3.1 – Roles of the players in the open source community.
(Adaptation from Feller & Fitzgerald, 2002)

	Customer	Actor	Decision-maker
Users	Use of OSS for personal or professional reasons.	Feedback to the community produced from actual use.	OSS quality assessment.
Prosumers	Use of OSS within the OSS development process.	Re-actor: stabilization of software. Pro-actor: addition of new features.	Influence on the direction development takes.
Leader Teams	Use of OSS within the OSS development process.	Product design. Integration of contributions.	Project management.
Companies	Internal use of open source products.	Partial contribution to OSS development.	Product diffusion and, sometimes, distribution.
Institutions	Internal use of open source products.	Involvement in the research and development of OSS (universities) and open standards (governments).	Specific investments in support of the community.

3.2 Demographics

We have just seen that the open source community is made up of a variety of stakeholders who, in different ways, support the community. This is a concept of community in a broad sense, but there is no doubt that the heart of the community is the development community. Prosumers are the most active players in the development community. Who are these people that dedicate a significant amount of their free time to developing open source software? In order to answer these questions we can look at the results of studies carried out by the Technical University of Berlin (TUB, 2001), the International Institute of Infonomics at the University of Maastricht (FLOSS, 2002) and The Boston Consulting Group in cooperation with the Open Source Development Network (BCG/OSDN, 2002).

Men or women? All three surveys confirm that the participation in the open source community is overwhelming male, about 98%.

How old are they? More than 70% were aged between 22 and 27 at the time of the study and are thus members of what is now commonly called Generation X, i.e. the generation of people born in the late 1960s and 1970s. (The term comes from Douglas Coupland's 1991 book *Generation X: Tales For An Accelerated Culture.*) The second largest group, about 16% of the total, consists of people born between 1945 and 1964, followed by members of the so-called Generation Y, i.e. people born in the 1980s.

What degrees do they have? The majority of open source software developers have a university (Bachelor's or Master's) degree, about a fifth have just a high school degree and fewer than 10% have a PhD. The members of this community do not seem to give significant importance to very high levels of education, i.e. post-graduate work.

What is their professional background? About 60% are IT professionals, e.g. programmer, software engineer, IT manager, and the second largest group is made up of people in academia (ca. 30%), two-thirds of whom are students.

Where do they come from/Where do they live? Over 80% live in North America and Europe. However, the data regarding the distribution of these people by nationality differs significantly in the three surveys considered: while the FLOSS study found 70% are from Europe and only 14% from North America, the BCG/OSDN survey and TUB study found a more equal distribution in North America and Europe.

How much time do they spend on developing OSS? The data from all three studies reveals that even though some professionals are now paid to work on OSS, participation in OSS projects continues to be mainly a hobby. From a third to a half spend less than 5 hours a week on OSS, about a third spend from 6 to 20 hours a week, about a tenth spend from 21 to 40 and only 5% spend more than 40 hours a week.

How many projects do they contribute to at the same time? According to the BCG/OSDN survey, 30% work on 1 project, 28% on 2 projects, 22% on 3 projects and 18% on 4 or more projects. The FLOSS survey reported similar percentages. Both surveys had respondents who were not currently working on an OSS project but who had in the past. About 80% of the developers work on at most 3 projects and the distribution from 1 project to 3 projects is relatively even.

How might these demographics change 10 or 20 years from now? Is it plausible to think that a community of young graduate males who dedicate their spare time to developing free software is sustainable? At present there is no reason to believe it is not. It is possible and reasonable to imagine that new generations, born in the Information Age, will continue to show an interest in open source software development. What might change is the geographical distribution. Developing countries, such as India and China, have a large population of potential contributors. The age distribution might change as well.

3.3 The Motivating Factors of Individuals and Organizations

The question Bill Gates asked in 1976 continues to be one of the most frequently asked questions when speaking about the open source community: who can afford to do professional work for nothing? In other words, what drives and motivates software developers, companies and organizations to invest their resources in activities which do not produce immediate profits?

In order to answer these questions, we must distinguish between individual software developers, organizations and society as a whole. Although these are all heterogenous groups, it is possible to identify motivating factors that the players in each group have in common. Open source can offer individuals, organizations and society benefits that motivate these groups to directly or indirectly participate in or support the community.

3.3.1 Motivations for individuals

As we have just seen, the majority of the software developers in the open source community are IT professionals or IT students who receive no financial compensation for their contributions. Furthermore, though the average amount of time they spend per week on open source projects is 5 hours, some spend up to 40 hours or more per week. So the question we pose here is what moves these people to dedicate their time, most often free time, to participating in this community. We will consider a well-known distinction between two types of motivation: "*intrinsic motivation*, which refers to doing something because it is inherently interesting or enjoyable, and *extrinsic motivation*, which refers to doing something because it leads to a separable outcome".[36] We will look at the extrinsic motivations first as they tend to be the more evident and 'tangible'.

Surveys have shown that one of the most important reasons respondents give for participating in an open source project is to improve their own technical knowledge base. Learning and improving one's performance tend to be ranked among the top reported reasons for contributing to open source projects.[37] Another high-ranking motivating factor is the so-called *scratching an itch phenomenon,* i.e. people participate in a project to solve a particular technical problem or satisfy specific technical needs. Furthermore, these people can exploit the contributions that the community can offer, such as independent peer review and feedback from the community regarding the quality of the work carried out. The so-called "Linus's Law", from Linus Torvalds, states that "given enough eyeballs, all the bugs are shallow", i.e. with a given number of users any problem can quickly be identified and pointed out.

The knowledge individuals gain by participating in projects or solving problems can lead to other extrinsic motivations which are more economic in nature. The fact that the source code is open increases the visibility of each individual's contribution. Therefore, not only is each programmer that much more responsible for his own contribution, but the fact that other programmers have access to it can improve one's own reputation within the community. The main motivating factor for software developers, from an economic point of view, is, in fact, to have their abilities recognized by the community (peer recognition) in order to increase their value as professionals in the job market. An improvement in reputation can lead to job offers and promotion, future career benefits and even paid consulting opportunities. The benefits gained by improving one's reputation can justify what voluntary participation costs software developers in terms of time, money and opportunities lost. [38]

It is worth pointing out, however, that economic motivations seem to be much less important than increased knowledge or improved reputation motivations. In the BCG survey, 93% of respondents mentions "increased knowledge base" as an important benefit of participating in the open source community, 50% "improved reputation", and 33% "new job offers". In the FLOSS study, about 75% responded that one of the reasons to join the community was to "learn and develop new skills" while only 4% cited "make money" as one of these reasons.

The intrinsic motivations seem to be just as, if not more, important as the extrinsic motivations for the software developers in the open source community. This explains and justifies the fact that so many professionals keep the community thriving even without financial compensation for the work they do. Linus Torvalds, the initiator of one of the most successful open source software projects (Linux), was not primarily motivated by reputation concerns, but rather by a desire to participate in a community he identified with. [39] In fact, surveys have shown that "self-determination", i.e. the feeling of accomplishment, competence, enjoyment and effectiveness, and enjoyment-based intrinsic motivation, i.e. the sense of creativity and intellectual stimulation experienced when working on an open source software project, are mentioned as two of the most important reasons for participating in the open source community. [40] These intrinsic motivating factors can be either personal or social in nature. For example, the second most important benefit of participating in an open source software project cited in the BCG/OSDN survey was "personal sense of accomplishment for contribution" and in the FLOSS survey about 60% answered "share knowledge and skills" as the reason they joined or continue to participate in the community.

Many open source software developers find working on open source software projects intellectually stimulating and participate for the pure creative satisfaction of doing so. The creation of a code can be considered a form of artistic production similar to musical composition or painting, where gratification and intellectual satisfaction play a fundamental role. [41] Paul Graham, author of *Hackers & Painters,* a book that examines the world of hackers and what motivates them, stated:

> When I finished grad school in computer science I went to art school to study painting. A lot of people seemed surprised that someone interested in computers would also be interested in painting. They seemed to think that hacking and painting were very different kinds of work – that hacking was cold, precise, and methodical, and that painting was the frenzied expression of some primal urge. Both of these images are wrong. Hacking and painting have a lot in common. In fact, of all the different types of people I've known, hackers and painters are among the most alike. What hackers and painters have in common is that they're both makers. Along with composers, architects, and writers, what hackers and painters are trying to do is make good things. [42]

What Graham is describing here is what Raymond has called the joy of hacking. It is "...the pure artistic satisfaction of designing beautiful software and making it work. Hackers all experience this kind of satisfaction and thrive on it". [43] Furthermore, the very way in which the community is organized creates an environment where people can express their creativity, have fun and feel a sense of accomplishment. Developers have the freedom to experiment in writing code and to choose the projects they are most interested in or that best suit their abilities.

In this context, it is not surprising that many members are also motivated by a belief that free and unlimited access to information must be guaranteed. They consider software to be a knowledge product and therefore a common good. Consequently, software should be freed from the restrictions imposed by copyright. They refuse to accept closed codes and above all the presence of monopolies. It is interesting to note that the results of the FLOSS study indicate that this sense of disapproval of proprietary software and monopolies increases once people have joined the open source community.

The factors that motivate software developers to participate in the open source community are summarized in Table 3.2.

Table 3.2 – Motivations for individuals' involvement in open source software projects.

Extrinsic Motivations for Individuals	Intrinsic Motivations for Individuals
Technical	Personal
Improve one's own technical knowledge base. Solve technical problems and satisfy personal needs related to software (*scratching an itch*). Exploit peer-review to improve a software product.	Personal sense of accomplishment for one's own contribution. Work on intellectually stimulating projects. Pure creative satisfaction (*joy of hacking*).
Economic	Social
Improved reputation (*signaling incentives*). Job offers/promotion and future career benefits. Paid consulting opportunities.	Sense of belonging to a community that fosters cooperation. Share knowledge and skills (*Gift culture and economy*). Oppose proprietary software and monopolies.

In a community where a significant proportion of the members participate for the joy of hacking, for intellectual stimulation or personal satisfaction, sharing and diffusing the results of one's own work become important. This philosophy is the basis on which a the open source community is built: gift economy.[44] In a gift economy, a person's social status depends more on how much he/she is willing and able to contribute and share information than how much he/she is able to have exclusive property of information. [45] As Raymond writes, "In gift cultures, social status is determined not by what you control but by *what you give away.*" (italics in original)[46]

3.3.2 Motivations for organizations

Companies and institutions also have important reasons for investing their time and money in observing the open source community, using open source software products, and/or participating in the development of open source software products. All of the motivating factors for commercial organizations that we will discuss can be considered extrinsic as they provide either indirect or direct benefits.

First of all, for companies the community is a sort of reservoir of a high-quality work force which is already productive. Companies can limit training costs by hiring people in the community who have already acquired skills and knowledge in a given area (*alumni effect*).

Open source products are usually high-quality technologically advanced products. Companies take advantage of the increased quality of these software products by choosing to use them. At the same time, the availability of source codes allows companies to increase the quality of the open source software they are using within their organization by modifying software products to suit their needs. These modifications would be impossible to carry out internally on products protected by copyright.

Some companies directly participate in the development of software in collaboration with the open source community. To be involved in development, the company must make technological and human resources available. This commitment, and the relative costs, must have an economic return which can obviously not come from sales. One motivating factor is the possibility this collaboration offers for limiting research and development costs. In fact, the effort required for these activities can be shared among the members of the entire development community. Though the results obtained in cooperation cannot be claimed by any single company, companies can exploit the results to the benefit of their own product quality and internal processes. A final motivating factor is that participating in open source software projects can help improve company image. This helps break the company image away from the profit making aspect and give customers the impression that the company is interested in improving quality and doing something useful for society.

3.3.3 Motivations for society

There are reasons why even society as a whole might support the open source community and benefit from the development of open source software products. Companies and institutions can benefit from the work of the open source community to contribute to the development of open standards and high-quality products even when there are other dominant proprietary products. Promoting open standards which are not the property of any single company can stimulate competition and lead to higher product quality, reliability and stability to the benefit of all members of society. Open source software is, therefore, also an effective means by which to oppose monopolies. Proprietary software, and in particular the dominant software of monopolies, is in complete contradiction with the belief that software should be available to everyone at a low cost. Open source products could also be used to limit the so-called *digital divide*, i.e. the technological gap between industrialized and developing countries. These products could be distributed in countries where a significant public debt and slow development make it difficult to invest in technology.

Table 3.3 summarizes the factors that motivate organizations and society to support and/or be involved in the open source community.

Table 3.3 – Motivations for the involvement of organizations and society in the open source community.

Motivations for organizations	Motivations for society
Find competent technical personnel. Increase software quality.	Exploit open standards to stimulate competition, lower costs and improve quality.
Take advantage of the open source community for research and development. Improve company image.	Oppose the power of monopolies. Have access to low-cost software. Limit the digital divide.

3.4 Organization of the Open Source Community

One might think that a community of program developers with different technical motivations would lead to an uncontrollable and chaotic situation. Nonetheless, this is not the case. Clearly then, the community is organized in some way. Although we might be stretching it to speak of the organizational "structure" of the open source community, we can identify characteristics that define how the community and development processes are organized.[47] From the organizational point of view, two distinctive characteristics are open participation and decentralized decision-making power. From the point of view of processes, two other characteristics are fast development and parallel development. These characteristics have come into being as the community has grown and evolved. We could even say that they have become rules that help avoid the generation of negative phenomena and guarantee stability and continuity over time and the quality of the results obtained.

Each of the characteristics has advantages and drawbacks. We will see what these are and how the open source community has found ways to limit the negative effects of the drawbacks (Figure 3.2).

Open participation is the premise for the other three characteristics, i.e. bottom-up organization, fast development and parallel development. Open participation makes it possible to explore different alternatives and

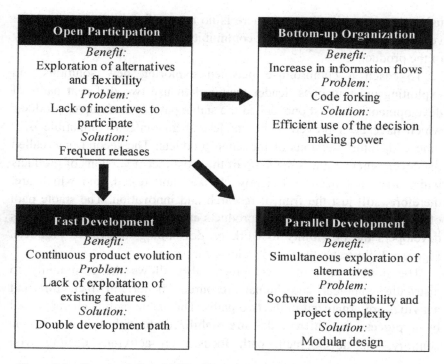

Figure 3.2 – Characteristics of the organization and development process in the open source community.

make strategies flexible. However, this makes it impossible to define precise deadlines in the development process. The non-specificity of objectives could lead to a lack of incentives for developers and little motivation to speed up development and make a strong commitment to it. The community overcomes this problem by creating numerous and frequent releases of the code to stimulate developers to actively contribute.[48]

Fast development and frequent releases create a continuous evolution of products. The advantage of continuously modifying and releasing products makes it possible to maintain technologically avant-garde products. However, innovation does not always guarantee total product reliability and stability, at least not until products have been sufficiently and thoroughly checked. This could discourage people from using these products because there is no reason for a user to use recent versions of a product when the community cannot guarantee the quality of the product.

To reach a compromise between exploring new solutions and exploiting existing ones, leader teams often use two different paths of development. The first one, called the stable path, is made up of products which have been proved to be stable and guaranteed compatible over time with future versions of the same products. The second one, called the development path, is made up of the most recent versions of products which have not been sufficiently checked and tested, and which are, therefore, still just the fruit of research and innovation. The stable path offers users reliable and tested products and the development path gives developers the possibility to work on developing innovative products. Figure 3.3 illustrates the two development paths.

The double path of development also allows the community to distribute technical and human resources better. In fact, different activities are organized in the two paths. The stable path is characterized by a process in which codes are stabilized through testing. On the contrary, the development path focuses on activities dealing with

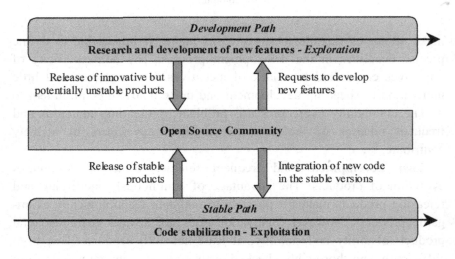

Figure 3.3 – The two development paths used in open source projects.

the research and development of new features. The creation of the two paths makes it possible to improve the distribution of the responsibilities and the organization of the activities. Nevertheless, stability and innovative research must always be carefully balanced. Therefore, the two paths must periodically be integrated with each other. This happens in an explicit way when new features and a new code are transferred from the development path to the stable path. This integration happens in an implicit way when feedback from the products in the stable path indicates new features that the development path should work on.

Parallel development is another advantage of open participation. The community has a theoretically unlimited number of volunteer developers at its disposal and can therefore allow them to work on different alternatives at the same time. This makes it possible to find the best solution in the shortest time possible. The disadvantage, however, is that contributions developed by different programmers at the same time may overlap, interfere and/or be incompatible making it difficult to manage development projects.

When software is produced in the traditional way, excessive parallelism is considered to be a waste of resources and a factor that increases the complexity of the development process. The well-known Brooks's Law states that as the number of software developers increases, there is a proportional increase in the amount of code produced but that there is also an increase in the complexity of the project proportional to the square of the number of software developers.[49] This complexity leads to higher communication and management costs and a greater possibility of making errors.

Brooks's Law is still widely accepted by companies, software developers and academics. Nonetheless, some large open source projects (e.g. the Linux and Apache projects) seem to demonstrate that the negative effects of Brooks's Law can at least be limited by using certain strategies. One such strategy is to divide relatively large/complicated products into more simple, mono-functional parts. In this way resources are used more efficiently and any interferences between single contributions are more easily solved. Modular product planning reduces the negative effects of Brooks's Law in that these effects can be traced to smaller portions of the code and more easily dealt with. The leader teams are responsible for the modularity of open source products. In fact, they plan products and guide the development of the interface protocol to be used for communication between the various modules. Modularity also means that additions, modifications and imperfections present in one module do not have negative effects on the whole code, but rather are limited to that one module.

Another strategy is to exploit the possibilities offered by the Internet to reduce communication and organization costs. Thanks to the connectivity offered by the Internet, software developers do not have to meet in a physical place to discuss and exchange ideas and codes. In particular, the community uses specific tools, such as the *Current Versioning System* (CVS), discussion forums and mailing lists, to manage parallelism. The CVS is basically a database containing the various contributions to the project, each of which is identified by a different name and date. This tool can help software developers eliminate the interferences and obstacles that cooperation naturally creates. The CVS is also useful in the debugging process because it makes it possible to track the development sequence and identify the exact point in the sequence where the defects are. A bug database makes it easier to identify and solve problems. When a new problem arises, programmers can quickly look for similar problems in the bug database to see what solutions have already been used. Together with discussion forums, the CVS is also used to archive all of the comments and questions that arise in the community during the development of projects.

A project mailing list should not be considered less important. Developers depend on mailing lists to stay in touch with one another and remain up to date on the evolution of projects. Furthermore, new entries can read the archived messages of a given mailing list to get familiarized with a project and become productive right away.

Bottom-up organization with no strict top-down planning is the third characteristic generated by open participation. This type of organization means that projects can be more flexible and have greater freedom to evolve. However, the negative side of flexible organization is code forking, i.e. a situation that occurs when independent development paths of a code dedicated to reaching the same goals fork off in different directions.[50]

Code forking can only be accepted if it leads to different features or the same product and cannot be accepted if it leads to the dispersion of contributions, incompatibility of versions and lack of communication between development teams. When peer review is not carried out, the positive effects of collaboration are reduced in terms of product quality, speed, and stability.

The consequences of code forking can be very serious. The loss of collaboration between the members of the community outweigh the positive effects of parallel development. If the community divides up into many subgroups, it could lose the number of programmers and users needed to maintain the fast speed of the product development process, or even worse, the community could implode. The community often loses interest in projects that are subject to code forking. This loss provokes the gradual but unstoppable process of developers distancing themselves from a project that is destined to eventually die. In fact, software developers will want to look elsewhere for a project which can offer the reputation and recognition that a project which risks failing because of code forking cannot.

Fortunately, the code forking phenomenon is very rare in the open source community. When code forking does happen, the community turns to its leader teams to help avoid project failure. Leaders must carefully listen to the opinions of the different members of the project and reach a consensus on the future of the project. They can make suggestions and indicate which direction the development processes should take. They also have to demonstrate the feasibility of projects and try to maintain software developers' interest in the project.

One way to help avoid code forking in large scale projects is to create a management structure made up of team leaders responsible for different parts of a project. By distributing authority among different teams, not only are their managerial responsibilities reduced, but their responsibilities are specific to one given module. In this way, it is easier to respond quickly to needs and to control better the development process. It is important to remember that the power of the leaders comes from the credibility and trust the community places in them. Credibility and trust mostly come from the value and importance of the contributions leaders have made. The leaders can maintain their position only so long as their decisions remain transparent and impartial and so long as they are able to demonstrate technical expertise.

Strong leadership, therefore, reduces the risk of code forking. In fact, any possible "rebel" factions would have to look for other leaders capable of attracting a large enough part of the community to work on a new project. An attempt like this is often made in vain in particular when the project has, as is the case with Linux, a recognized and indisputable leader.

The community also has two other strategies to protect itself from behaviours that can harm the community. Flaming and shunning are the reaction strategies the community can use against anyone, be he/she a leader or programmer, who threatens to break the social rules of the community. Flaming is the public condemnation of the guilty party. Shunning, on the other hand, isolates the "hijacker", i.e. refuses to cooperate with the guilty party. In other words, the guilty party is forced out of the open source development community.

To sum up, the community tries to avoid code forking and any other negative behaviours by whatever means necessary since it sees this phenomenon as a risk to the survival of its projects and to the community itself.

In this chapter we have seen who makes up the open source community and how it works. Although it might be possible to consider the way in which open source software is developed to be a new model for software development, open source software is currently only a small part of all of the software developed. The proprietary model for software development is much more widely used and will most likely continue to be so in the future. Therefore, it is worth comparing these two different ways of developing software in order to understand their respective strengths and weaknesses. Can the so-called open source model become a new and superior software development model? In the next chapter, we will try to answer this question by taking a look at the evolution of software development models and then comparing them with the open source model.

Chapter 4

Software Development Models

Software has many characteristics that make it very different from more traditional products. First and foremost, software is in a digital format; it is not a physical product. This makes it difficult to define and quantify the quality of software using quantitative parameters. Secondly, it is complex since it has to interact with hardware and other software systems on a computer. Thirdly, software, unlike many industrial products, must evolve at a very rapid pace. Developers must constantly update and improve the characteristics of a software product in order to meet the many needs of users and the advances made in the other technologies software interacts with. Fourthly, software today must be user-friendly; if it isn't, people won't use it. Finally, in the case of software, more than in the case of traditional products, the quality of the development processes determines the quality of the final product. Therefore, in order to guarantee the quality of a software products, it is indispensable to correctly define, plan and manage the development processes.

This complexity and uniqueness led to the development of a new discipline in the field of software development to study how the development processes of software products can be defined and evaluated. This discipline, called Software Engineering[51], deals with the activities involved in planning, building and maintaining software.

In this chapter we will take a look at the various consolidated software development models. This analysis will allow us to then compare these consolidated processes with those used by Open Source.

4.1 The Software Development Process

In general, the software development process can be divided into five stages, which can also be considered problem solving activities: defining the product and analyzing requirements, planning the system, developing and testing the subsystems, integrating and testing the system, and using the system and maintenance.[52]

The first stage involves deciding what needs users have and identifying which competences and resources are currently available or not. Several different possible solutions are identified and evaluated.

During the second stage, the components, modules and structures that together will make up the entire software system are formally identified. In other words, the overall architecture of the product is planned. During this stage, the development process is planned as well.

In the third stage, the code is developed following the design specifications that have previously been determined. In this stage, each single component is tested, not the system as a whole, and often the focus is on analyzing whether or not the code is correct.

The development process is completed during the fourth stage by integrating the single parts into one whole product (internal integration) and checking the interactions and possible interferences and incompatibility between the components and systems external to the product (external integration). Integration involves intense testing that must be able to check the efficiency and quality of the product as a whole and in its interaction with other systems.

Since the development process formally ends in the fourth stage, the fifth stage involves all of the follow-up activities that take place once a product has reached the market. Some of these activities are customer assistance and product maintenance. Since, product maintenance activities are usually very significant from an economic point of view, they must be considered a part of the development process.

The degree to which each of these five stages are carried out in a thorough and correct way determines the nature of the development process implemented. Therefore, these activities are the variables that must be considered when choosing a development model.

4.2 Software Development Process Models

We will now give a brief description of the main system development process models. By considering them in the chronological order, we will highlight how the disadvantages of each model led to the development of new models that tried to improve on the drawbacks of the previous one.[53] The primary approaches are: Build and Fix Model, Waterfall Model, Iterative Process, Evolutionary Model, and Spiral Model. Finally, we will take a more thorough look at a particularly important model: Microsoft's Synch and Stabilize.

4.2.1 The Build and Fix Model

Build and Fix, or Ad-hoc Development, was the first model used by early software developers before software engineering became a discipline. The name itself describes the rather haphazard way in which software is developed using this model. The five problem solving steps involved in developing software are not carried out in any particular order. The project specifications and system requirements don't have to be evaluated or defined in a formal way. In fact, the quality of the results of Ad-hoc development depend entirely on the skills and experience of the individual staff members working on the project. These characteristics led the Software Engineering Institute to define the Build and Fix model "unpredictable". The dependence on staff members means that the loss of members with key skills usually has very negative effects on the development process.

From an economic point of view the model is risky. Testing is usually carried out only at the end of the development process on versions of a complete product. Modifications are then most often made at the end of the development process after the product has been released.

Nonetheless, this model continues to be used today for small projects or products that are expected to have a time-limited use. The model is not suitable to complex or long-term projects that depend more on organizational capability rather than solely on the capabilities of individuals.

4.2.2 The Waterfall Model

The Waterfall Model was the first development model to be defined according to some of the basic principles of software engineering and the first to formally structure the development process. The entire life-cycle of a product is divided into six steps. The first four make up the formal development process, whereas the fifth step involves actual use of the product and the sixth one withdrawal from the market.

- *Systems Analysis.* In this step as much information as possible is gathered regarding system requirements and performances required by users.
- *System Design.* This step involves the precise and formal definition of how the system will be constructed to perform the requirements identified in the previous step. The development process is planned in detail as well.
- *Coding and Module Testing.* Each part of the code is programmed and tested separately from the rest of the system
- *Integration and System Testing.* This is the last step in the formal development process. All of the parts of the code are integrated and tested to make sure it can perform the necessary functions efficiently. The final version of the product is built.
- *Deployment and Use.* The product is deployed and used in real-life conditions. Users provide feedback that makes it possible to propose new functions that can be a part of the next development cycle.
- *Discontinue the Product.* The product is withdrawn form the market and resources are assigned to other projects.

The Waterfall method can be considered linear since the steps are clearly separated from one another and follow each other in a precise order (Figure 4.1). Even the way feedback is used preserves the linearity of the model. Though there is feedback at each step in the cycle, it is not considered at the end of each step but rather gathered and considered all together at the end of the cycle. These considerations are then used to make modifications in the system requirements, starting a new cycle.

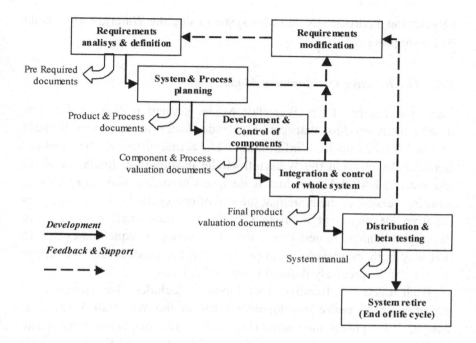

Figure 4.1 – The Waterfall Model.

The Waterfall Model calls for a series of documents that follow the evolution of the development process. They describe the process in detail and can be used to plan future projects. The process becomes repeatable and is thus less susceptible to difficulties that arise from the changes in staff. Furthermore, defining standard procedures is the first step in improving processes and, consequently, product quality.

The main drawback to this model is the need to determine the system requirements in detail from the beginning of the process. In the case of software, there is often a great deal of uncertainty about requirements and goals on both the part of users and developers. Unexpected changes, which are quite common, can create significant development and financial setbacks. The more innovative a project is, the greater these risks become. Therefore, the Waterfall Model is mostly used when the requirements for a system are either known or easily identifiable.

Developing a particularly complex system using the Waterfall Model can be a long process.

4.2.3 The Iterative Development Model

The rigid nature of the Waterfall Model created a demand for new development models that could provide faster results even without precise, detailed up-front information. The actual difference between the Iterative Process and the Waterfall Model is subtle but fundamental. In the Waterfall Model a product is designed in such a way as to yield a working version of the system at the end of one cycle. On the contrary, in Iterative Development a product is divided into small parts that are developed in an incremental way through a series of sequential cycles. In this way both the development process and the product architecture do not have to be precisely defined from the beginning.

Each cycle in Iterative Development includes the sequence of activities of an entire development cycle in the Waterfall Model, i.e. design, development and testing (Figure 4.2). Iterative Development can, in fact, be considered a sort of waterfall of waterfalls. Each cycle produces a partially-usable product that can be tested to obtain feedback needed for the improvement and evolution of the product. Each new

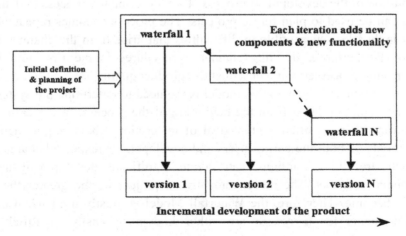

Figure 4.2 – Iterative Development.

release incrementally improves on or broadens the functions developed in the preceding cycles. Results are obtainable earlier on in the process and valuable feedback can be obtained and used to modify requirements and make improvements throughout the process.

The drawback to this approach is that it can be afflicted by scope creep, i.e. the subtle but pervasive increase in the scope of a project that significantly alters the original design and estimates of resources. Incremental development and constant feedback can lead developers to continuously conceive of and introduce new functions to complete a product. This can, in turn, lead to excessive instability in a project and inefficiency.

To sum up, Iterative Development is suitable for highly innovative products. In these projects, the initial requirements are not precisely known and it is impossible to foresee the future evolution of the project.

4.2.4 The Evolutionary Model

The Evolutionary Model is an improvement on the Iterative Process. It introduces the concept of concurrent development cycles. In other words, whereas in Iterative Development cycles are repeated in a sequence, in the Evolutionary Model several cycles take place at the same time and the beginning of one cycle does not necessarily depend on the completion of a previous one.

As can be seen in Figure 4.3 the product must first be divided into modules that can be developed autonomously. Then, concurrent, or overlapping, cycles are carried out for the same module. This can provide useful information earlier on in the process before the problem solving cycle is completed. At the same time, this process is duplicated for the development of the other modules, i.e. the parallel development of different modules. Once the different modules have been developed and tested, they are then integrated in the complete system.

The advantage of the Evolutionary Model is that it leads to significant reductions in the time it takes to complete a project. However, there is the risk that the modules, when integrated, will be incompatible. This type of development requires sophisticated coordination able to manage the various development cycles and guarantee compatibility.

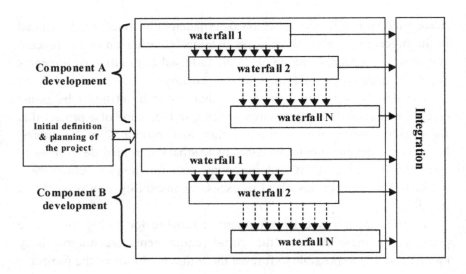

Figure 4.3 – The Evolutionary Model.

4.2.5 The Prototyping Model

As we have already pointed out, one of the challenges in software development is that users are often not able to supply correct and detailed information about what they want. This makes it difficult for software designers to adequately define the system requirements and product specifications at the beginning of the development process. The Prototyping Model was developed to overcome the problem of limited up-front information.

When using the Prototyping Model, the developer builds a simplified version of a product (a prototype) in the early stages of the development process in order to receive feedback on it. The developers and customers use the prototype, evaluate it and provide feedback. The developer then refines the system requirements and development process in response to the information provided. If necessary, the prototype code can be thrown away and an entirely new one developed. This is plausible from a financial point of view because the prototype does not necessarily have to be a real system. The prototype can be a simulation of the system and its main interfaces without any substantial coding or an abbreviated version of the system that performs a limited subset of functions. This makes it possible to obtain feedback without having to develop all of the functions of a product.

The Prototyping Model divides the development process into two distinct parts: development of the prototype and development of the actual product. The main advantage of this process is that it reduces the risks of development, especially for innovative projects. Receiving important information early on helps save time and money. However, prototyping can lead to poorly designed systems. Decisions taken when considering the prototype, which has been developed quickly, may be incorrect when dealing with the real system.

4.2.6 The Spiral Model

The Spiral Model was designed to include the best features from the Iterative, Evolutionary and Prototyping Models, and introduces a new feature which is particularly important in the case of software – risk-assessment. The model proposes the continuous repetition of cycles (Iterative Model) and overlapping of the design, development and testing steps in each cycle (Evolutionary Model). An initial version of the system is developed to gather the information needed to start the iterative and parallel development of modules (Prototyping Model). Risk assessment is included as a step in each cycle of the development process. Risk involves the uncertainty of the results of each cycle. This uncertainty can come from a lack of information regarding system requirements, inadequately skilled staff and inaccurate scheduling and budgeting. Each cycle produces a version of the product that is evaluated in order to determine whether or not development should continue.

The Spiral Model is suitable to the dynamic nature of software development and the need to have a very flexible process. The initial design is not specified in detail, but rather is kept flexible. The approach is no longer sequential, but rather, as the name itself says, follows a cyclical path creating a spiral as the development of the system takes place[54] (Figure 4.4). The spiral starts at the centre and develops outward. The size of the spiral, i.e. the distance from the centre, represents the increase in the costs of the development process, in the complexity and

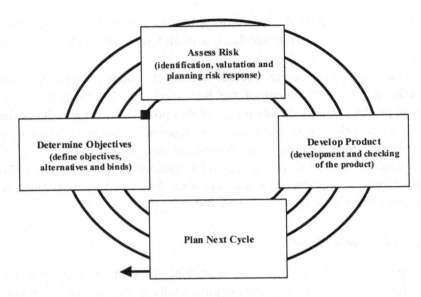

Figure 4.4 – The Spiral Model.

completeness of the versions of the system and in the effort required to carry out risk assessment.[55] Since the consequences of undesired events are greater as the project grows, risks must be considered, evaluated and managed from the start of the project. By doing so, this model makes it possible to more quickly identify and eliminate risks and errors and ensure a higher quality project.

The complexity of the Spiral Model is both its strong point and its weak point. Implementation of this model requires skilled and experienced people and adequate financial resources. Microsoft's "Synch and Stabilize" Model is a Spiral Model.

4.3 Classification and Comparison of the Models

The system development process models so far discussed can be considered consolidated as they are all part of the specific body of knowledge of software engineering. The characteristics of these models and their strong and weak points in the following two tables.

Table 4.1 – Comparison of consolidated system development process models.

Models / Criteria	Build and Fix	Waterfall	Iterative	Evolutionary	Prototyping	Spiral
Possibility to repeat the process	No	Yes	Yes	Yes	Yes	Yes
Ability to deal with innovation	No	No	Yes	Yes	Yes	Yes
Capability to cope with changes in requirements	Limited	Limited	Sufficient	Very good	Very good	Very good
Ability to cope with complex projects	Limited	Limited	Sufficient	Sufficient	Very good	Very good
Need to have up-front information	Necessary	Necessary	Preferable	Preferable	Not necessary	Not necessary
Risk management	No	No	Partial	Partial	Partial	Yes

In Table 4.1, the models are compared according to the following criteria:

- *Possibility to repeat the process.* This criteria is directly related to the degree of formalization and planning of the development process.
- *Ability to deal with innovation.* This depends on whether or not the tools and skills needed for development are available.
- *Capability to cope with changes in requirements.* This is determined by how easily the model can adapt to changes in requirements during the development cycle.
- *Ability to cope with complex projects.* Complexity depends on the competences required, the degree of innovation and the number of modules that make up the complete product.

- *Need to have detailed up-front information.* This means that the development process cannot start without defined requirements and specifications.
- *Risk-management.* This regards the model's ability to assess risk during the development process.

Table 4.1 highlights the fact that, starting from the Build and Fix model, the models improve more and more until they reach the most complete model, the Spiral Model. According to the evaluation criteria used, the only difference between the Build and Fix Model and the Waterfall Model is that the former is not repeatable. Both models are almost only effective for the development of systems that are well-defined and not very dynamic. This limitation depends on the intrinsic simplicity and limited formalization of the Build and Fix Model and on the excessive rigidity and formality of the Waterfall Model.

The Iterative Model introduces the possibility to cope with new technologies and competences since the incremental evolution it follows makes it possible to gradually add new requirements throughout the development process. The Evolutionary Model introduces parallelism, which speeds up the time it takes the model to react to new project requirements. The Prototyping Model is the first model able to cope well with complex projects and to not require detailed up-front information. And finally, the Spiral Model fully integrates risk management in the development process.

Another way to compare these models is by considering the strong and weak points of each model. Table 4.2 sums up the advantages and drawbacks of these models.

Now that we have a better understanding of what models are used in more traditional, commercial software development, we can compare them to the open source software development process. First we will take a more detailed look at one consolidated model in particular – Microsoft's Synch and Stabilize Model. We will then see what similarities and differences there are between this model and the development model used in the open source community.

Table 4.2 – Strong and weak points of the system development models.

Models	Strong Points	Weak Points
Build and Fix	Suitable for small projects that do not involve significant updating.	Unable to deal with complex projects. Processes are not repeatable and depend on the skills and experience of the project staff.
Waterfall	Formal approach based on documentation making it possible to repeat development processes.	The first usable version of the product is produced only at the end of a very long cycle.
Iterative	The process quickly produces a usable version of the product.	The process of interpreting and reacting to feedback is slow.
Evolutionary	The concurrent development of single modules and the parallel development of more than one module make it possible to quickly use feedback obtained throughout the development process.	Parallel development can lead to incompatibility.
Prototyping	The use of a prototype makes it easier to identify system requirements.	Mistakes made when evaluating the prototype can potentially reduce the quality of the final product.
Spiral	Risk assessment offers greater guarantees in terms of product quality and process efficiency (scheduling and budgeting).	Effective risk assessment requires skills and experience.

4.4 The Microsoft Model: Synch and Stabilize

Microsoft's system development process model is called Synch and Stabilize and is basically a personalization of the Spiral Model. The Synch and Stabilize Model involves the continuous synchronization of development activities and the periodic stabilization of products.[56] It is based on a few fundamental principles: 1 – evolution of specifications throughout the process; 2 – modularity; 3 – concurrent development.

The first principle is based on the concept that the project specifications are not "frozen" during the planning stage, but rather evolve throughout the whole development process. The second basic principle is modularity. Microsoft has begun to introduce the concept of modularity in particular for products that have a fast life cycle. The third principle is that the development activities and testing are iterated and carried out simultaneously during the development process. To sum up, "[…] the basic idea is that user needs for many types of software are so difficult to understand that is nearly impossible or unwise to try to design the system completely in advance, especially as hardware improvements and customer desires are constantly and quickly evolving. Instead project should iterate as well as concurrently manage as many design, build, and testing activities as possible while they move forward to complete a product." [57]

In the Microsoft development process there are three main phases that are repeated in each cycle of the spiral: planning, development and stabilization.

At the beginning of the planning phase, a general product concept is defined that specifies the main product functions. Customer input is used to identify and prioritise product functions and features. Assigning priority is an important aspect of Synch and Stabilize since Microsoft tends to reduce to a minimum the number of functions developed at the same time during a given cycle in the spiral. The definition of priorities is based on systematic activity based planning. Only the characteristics that are considered useful and appealing to customers are developed. This makes it possible to concentrate work on a limited number of functions and avoid wasting time and energy.

Once specifications have been defined, a specification document is drawn up that formally defines the functions, architecture and interdependencies between the components. The development activities are then planned using a feature driven product organization and development approach.[58] Functional teams are created and then divided into smaller feature teams responsible for developing the different product features. Each feature team is made up of approximately 1 program manager, 3-8 developers and 3-8 testers. The number of developers and testers is the same since they work on the code in parallel. This organization makes it possible for the various activities to take place in parallel since each individual team can work on different parts of the product.

The development phase is usually subdivided into 3 sequential subprojects each of which produces what's called a milestone release. This division makes the process more flexible and open to any changes that may be found to be necessary during the development of the product. At the end of each subproject there is a period of buffer time during which programmers can reflect on the work that has been carried out and, even more importantly, solve any unexpected problems that have come up.

Each day the codes produced are synchronized creating a 'daily build', which is a single release that brings together the individual work of each member of the team. In this way, each programmer is responsible for his/her own work and for the compatibility between his/her work and that of the other team members.

The fact that the teams are made up of not only programmers but testers as well makes it possible to start checking and evaluating codes from the first stages of development. When corrections to the code must be made, intervening immediately during the early stages of development produces better results. Since most programming errors are spotted right away, they do not propagate throughout the cycle slowing down development and increasing the costs of stabilizing the product.

In the stabilization phase the main components and characteristics of the product do not evolve. What takes place is called the "virtual freeze", i.e. product features are frozen. Two different testing campaigns take place during this phase: internal and external testing. During internal testing, thorough testing of the complete product is carried out by company personnel. This is followed by external testing or *beta testing*. External testing makes it possible to highlight the actual performance of a product since the code is tested in real use conditions. A sufficient number of beta tester such as OEMs (Original Equipment Manufacturers), ISVs (Independent Software Vendors) and end-users, who use the product for a given period of time. Should the product not be approved, a new development cycle is started with the aim of fixing the defects and malfunctioning identified during testing.

At the end of the entire development process, i.e. the last cycle in the spiral, the final release, or "gold master copy" is prepared and sent to manufacturing.

4.5 Comparison between Synch and Stabilize and the Open Source Software Development Process

The very characteristics that determine how the open source community works, e.g. open participation and bottom-up organization, make it impossible to identify a precise, standardized open source software development process model. Nonetheless, we can find various similarities between how the open source community develops software and the "cathedral style" models we have discussed so far.[59] These similarities are summed up and compared in Table 4.3.

Table 4.3 – Similarities between consolidated software development models and the open source development process.

Build and Fix	Importance of human resources and the knowledge and skills of individual programmers.
Waterfall	Focus on customer requirements; the importance of testing products on customers is recognized.
Iterative	Division of the project into subprojects; incremental development of functions and features.
Evolutionary	Concurrent development of each module and, at the same time, the parallel development of different modules in order to speed up the development process.
Prototyping	Importance of feedback in order to better understand user requirements and better define specifications.
Spiral	Synthesis of the strong points of the other models.

The development of open source software is based on the community of voluntary and independent software developers. A lot of importance is given to human resources, i.e. each programmer's knowledge and skills, just as in the Build and Fix model. End-users are involved in the development process as well by providing important feedback. This involvement means that particular attention is given to user requirements, as is the case in the Waterfall Model and all of those that followed. The development community then uses feedback to more accurately define product specifications and produce frequent releases, as is the case in the Prototyping Model.

Large-scale open source projects are managed using modularity. The overall project is carefully divided into subprojects and the various functions and features are developed in an incremental (Iterative Model) and concurrent (Evolutionary Model) way. The parallel development of different modules (Evolutionary Model) also speeds up the development process.

Overall, we can see that the open source community has taken advantage of the strong points of existing development process models. The way software is developed in this community is becoming more and more similar to the way it is developed using the Spiral Model. Nonetheless, we will see that there are some significant differences as well.

In order to compare the open source development process with the Spiral model, it might be more useful to compare the way in which the Linux project was developed with Microsoft's Synch and Stabilize Model. It is interesting to note how similar the two methods are. Two characteristics they have in common are modularity and parallel development. However, the way and degree to which they are implemented in the two models is quite different.[60] Table 4.4 highlights the main differences between the development process used for Open Source Linux and Microsoft's Synch and Stabilize model.

The development of the Linux operating system is based on an extremely modular planning of the code. Each single part is designed to carry out in the best and most simple way one single function. Modularity is indispensable for the decentralized parallel development that characterizes the project since it facilitates controlling parts of the code already developed and introducing new parts.

Table 4.4 – Comparison between the development process of the open source project
Linux and Microsoft's Synch and Stabilize model.

	Linux Development (Open source project)	Synch and Stabilize (Microsoft)
Use of modularity	Extensive Makes it easier to manage parallel development.	Limited Integrated approach has commercial advantages but limits parallel development.
Parallel Development	Extensive Makes it possible to quickly integrate new ideas and developments into the development process.	Limited New ideas and developments are integrated more slowly.
Testing	Open to the community Extensive testing in real life circumstances leads to greater product robustness and stability.	Beta testing Limited testing reduces the possibility to verify product reliability.

The fact that Microsoft now uses object-based programming languages demonstrates that it is trying to implement a certain degree of modularity into the development of its own products. Nonetheless, in most cases, Microsoft continues to prefer developing code in an integrated way. The integral approach to product development involves linking different parts of the source code during the final stages of the development process without carrying out preventive modular design during the initial stages. The reason Microsoft uses this strategy is basically commercial in nature. The integral approach makes it easy to distribute and sell different products bundled together into one package. The commercial advantages are counterbalanced by disadvantages in managing projects. In other words, integration makes it difficult to organize decentralized parallel development.

Another important difference deals with the concept of parallelism. For Microsoft parallelism is synonymous to redundancy and limited optimization of programmers' efforts. In fact, having two or more development teams working on the same part of code is considered a waste of resources. Vice versa, in the Linux development community, parallelism is considered an advantage. Overlapping programmers' efforts is plausible in this context since none of them are being paid to develop open source code. Furthermore, parallelism makes it possible to explore different solutions to the same problem and find the best possible solution in the least time necessary.

In the Microsoft model teams have to respect the deadlines decided on during the planning stage. In most cases, if a new idea is thought of after the planning stage, it cannot be taken into consideration until the planning stage of the following cycle. This is what happens regardless of whether the idea comes from the development team or from the outside. On the other hand, in the Linux project new ideas can be taken into consideration in one of two ways: the development process can be interrupted and started again from scratch to include the new ideas or other members of the community can start a process of parallel development. New ideas can come from anyone in the community just as anyone can decide to become involved in implementing new ideas. This strategy allows the Linux community to speed up product development in a way that Microsoft cannot since it is limited by the need to precisely plan a project's development cycles.

Both models recognize the importance of user feedback and exploit it to guarantee product quality. Microsoft has developed a series of initiatives to promote product testing not only within the company but by carrying out testing outside of the company as well. Microsoft's beta-testing is carried out by a limited group of people the company has selected. However, the beta-testers do not have access to the source code. This means that product testing and revision cannot be as fast and thorough as they are in the open source community. Since it is an open source product, Linux is distributed with the source code and this allows skilled users to more thoroughly and accurately evaluate the software. Furthermore, Linux is tested by real users in real conditions.

Finally, during the planning stage, Microsoft identifies the requirements of a generic user because its intention is to create products that can satisfy the majority of its potential customers. Consequently, during the development process, the particular characteristics or configurations of specific needs are not taken into consideration. Furthermore, the possibility of users being able to continuously configure products is not even considered. The choice to neglect the specific requirements of a limited number of users is determined by the need to limit costs. On the contrary, the Linux project does not have to consider costs since the programmers are volunteers. No particular type of user is identified as part of the Linux project. The availability of source code allows members of the community to autonomously solve problems or adapt the code to different needs.

Chapter 5

Open Source Products and Software Quality

In the last chapter we saw that the software development models used by commercial software companies are very structured as opposed to the open source development process which is much less structured. A question that might arise then is whether or not this unstructured model can produce the same quality of software that traditional models produce. In other words, are open source software products high quality products? The success of many OSS products so far would seem to indicate that they are. However, popularity and success cannot be the only factors taken into account when evaluating the quality of software. In fact, the most commonly used model for evaluating software quality considers many other types of criteria. But this leads us to another question: can the same criteria be used to evaluate software developed using two very different models? This chapter starts with a closer look at the actual projects and products the open source community has worked on and is currently working on. Then, from a more general discussion of how the quality of software is commonly evaluated we will see if these methods can or cannot be applied to open source software.

5.1 Open Source Software Projects

In order to better understand what different types of open source products there are, it might first be useful to take a look at some of the projects the open source community is working on. To do this we will use a classification made by Freshmeat, an organization that maintains a database of and offers news on open source products. Freshmeat classifies open source products according to various criteria, the most important of which are: software category, programming language used, the operating system the project refers to, and the license used.[61]

The software category classification is interesting because it allows us to see which type of software products the community focuses its development efforts on. Table 5.1 shows the total number of projects catalogued by Freshmeat for each software category and the percentage these projects make up out of the total number of projects.

Table 5.1 – Open source projects according to software category.
(Source: Freshmeat, July 2005)

Software Categories	Number of projects	%
Software Development	10689	16,20
System	10253	15,54
Internet	10184	15,43
Multimedia	6210	9,41
Communications	5676	8,60
Utilities	3037	4,60
Games/Entertainment	2700	4,09
Scientific/Engineering	2682	4,06
Text Processing	2407	3,65
Desktop Environment	2350	3,56
Office/Business	2055	3,11
Database	2017	3,06
Security	1586	2,40
Information Management	1250	1,89
Education	891	1,35
Text Editors	646	0,98
Terminals	318	0,48
Other/Nonlisted Topic	258	0,39
Printing	227	0,34
Documentation	170	0,26
Artistic Software	161	0,24
Home Automation	78	0,12
Adaptive Technologies	51	0,077
Religion	50	0,076
freshmeat.net	29	0,044
Total	65975	100

We can divide the software categories into three large groups. The first group is made up of projects that work on internet products (e.g. Apache), systems (e.g. operating systems such as GNU/Linux), and tools for software development (e.g. programming languages such as PHP and Perl). This group makes up a little less than half (48.3%) of all the open source projects. In the second group there are projects that focus on developing multimedia products and communication software. These projects make up 18.3% of the total. All of the other categories put together make up 33.4% of the total. This data highlights the fact that the open source community tends to focus on products that can be technological platforms rather than on specific application programs. A particularly striking example of this is the fact that office and business application programs make up a very small part of the total number of projects (2.8%).

Freshmeat has also classified what it considers to be the 20 best projects based on popularity, vitality and project rating. Popularity is based on number of subscriptions, URL hits and record hits, vitality on age of project, number of announcements and date of last announcement, and project rating on user ratings. At the time this book is being released for publication, the most popular project is Mplayer, a Linux application program for playing movies, Postfix, a messaging software, is first place in terms of vitality, and the Linux kernel is first place in terms of project rating. Nonetheless, it is important to point out that these classifications can change quite rapidly.

According to the classification based on programming languages used to develop projects, the predominant language used is C and Perl is the second most used language. Perl, PHP and Python are programming languages that have been developed solely and entirely within the context of open source projects. On the other hand, C, C++ and Java are available in both proprietary and open source versions. In other words, a significant number of open source projects are developed using programming languages that were developed by the open source community itself.

Another classification of open source projects can be made based on the operating systems the software being developed runs on. The development community prefers open source operating systems and

POSIX in particular. The POSIX category includes GNU/Linux, BSD Linux, and the Linux versions developed by SUN Microsystems, HP and others. More than half of the preferences go to the original GNU/Linux and nearly 20% are for the BSD Linux whereas only the remaining 20% of the preferences go to the other versions. In other words, the community seems to prefer working with the original open source versions of Linux. Furthermore, this preference shows that within the community there is still quite a bit of diffidence with regards to the direct involvement of large companies in the development of open source software that carries the brand name of the company involved. The second largest category is multi-platform software. Software is called multi-platform when it is compatible with different environments, i.e. when it can be executed regardless of the specific operating system used by the user. This confirms the importance the community gives to the portability of open source products. Finally, the number of projects aimed at running on proprietary operating systems, i.e. Microsoft, Unix and Mac, make up slightly more than 20% of the total.

A final classification worth considering is the one regarding the licenses the various open source projects use. A large majority has chosen the GPL (GNU General Public License). Among those used less, the most popular ones are the LPGL (GNU Lesser General Public License) and the BSD License. Both of these licenses, as is the case of the GPL, were developed within the context of free/open source software specifically for these types of products. The proprietary licenses that come close to respecting the open source definition but do not completely respect it are not very diffused. For example, public domain software and freeware make up a very small percentage of the total. The reason why the vast majority of projects prefer to use the GPL is most likely that this license offers the greatest guarantees that the open source software will not become proprietary software. The open source community considers the GPL the best way to protect its work from free riders intent on creating private property from products developed by the community. Another possible explanation may simply be that the large number of products that already use the GPL induces new projects to use it as well.

5.2 Open Source Software Products

The projects we have just discussed are of interest to software developers and active members of the open source community, but not to most end-users. End-users are more interested in the concrete results of these projects, i.e. open source software products. Therefore, it is worth considering what OSS solutions are actually available. To do this, it might be helpful to classify these software products into four categories: system software, middleware, application software and programming languages.

To better understand what these different types of software are, it is useful to imagine a structure where system software is at the base, application software at the top, and as the name indicates, middleware in the middle. System software manages the computer's hardware resources and supports middleware and application software. It is independent of any specific type of application software. A computer's operating system is system software. Middleware is software that acts as an intermediary between different applications that have to interact. Middleware is also called *plumbing* because it connects two applications and passes data between them. Examples of middleware are web servers and database management systems. Application software is what end-users think of when they use the word software. In other words, it is software that performs specific tasks, e.g. word processing, graphics and spreadsheets. Programming languages are software used to develop all of the types of software in our structure. There are open source products in each of these categories (Table 5.2).

The following paragraphs summarize the information in the table and, when necessary, give a brief description of what these different types of software are:

System software The two most famous and widely used open source operating systems are GNU/Linux and FreeBSD. Both systems are based on the proprietary UNIX operating system and are proving to be quite competitive with other proprietary operating systems such as UNIX and Microsoft Windows.

Table 5.2 – Open source software products.

Category	Type of software	Example
System software	Operating systems	Linux FreeBSD
Middleware	Mail server software	Sendmail Qmail
	Web server software	Apache
	Application server software	Zope Jboss
	Data Base Management Systems	MySQL PostGreSql
	Protocols	Samba OpenLDAP OpenSSH
Application software	Office suites	OpenOffice Koffice
	Desktop environments	Gnome KDE
	Web browsers	Mozilla Firefox
	Management systems	Compiere
	Project management software	Achievo
	Groupware	Phprojekt
Programming languages		Perl PHP Python

Middleware The following products fall into this category: mail server software, web server software, application server software, database management systems and protocols.

- A mail server routes and delivers electronic mail messages and interacts with the application programs we use to manage our mail. The open source product Sendmail is the mail server software used to send more than fifty percent of all the e-mail in the world.

- A web server is a computer that delivers web pages to clients. Clients use a web browser to request information, the browser sends the request to the server which finds the requested information and sends it back to the browser where the user can see it. The open source web server software Apache is the most popular HTTP web server on the Internet, surpassing all other proprietary web servers.

- An application server is the computer in a computer network that runs certain centrally served software applications. The concept of application server is a return to the original model of computing where a central computer containing application software was accessed by multiple users whose computers ran software only for basic functions. The idea is to create lightweight network computers and avoid problems such as application integration. The use of application servers is still relatively limited. Two very popular open source application server software products are Zope and JBoss.

- A database management system (DBMS) is a suite of programs used to store information and act as a link to users who wish to access and modify the information stored. MySQL and PostGreSql are examples of open source DBMS software.

- Protocols are used to codify data so that it can be transmitted between two computing endpoints; they can be implemented in hardware or software. Samba and OpenLDAP are open source protocols.

Application software This is the category of software products that most users are familiar with because it includes the user-friendly products we interact with every day. The software that falls into this category includes: office suites, desktop environments, web browsers, management systems, project management software and groupware.

- Office suites are packages of several different applications that are bundled together. OpenOffice.org can be considered the open source version of Microsoft Office. It includes applications for creating and managing documents, spreadsheets, presentations, graphics and simple databases. KOffice is an open source office suite with features similar to those of OpenOffice.org, but designed specifically for the K Desktop Environment (KDE).

- The desktop environment is the graphical user interface you interact with when using a computer. Both GNOME and KDE are easy-to-use open source desktop environments for UNIX and UNIX-like operating systems.
- A web browser is the software that communicates with a web server to allow users to interact with documents hosted on the web server. Mozilla Firefox is an open source cross-platform Internet web browser.
- A management system is software for businesses. There are generally two types: Enterprise Resource Planning (ERP) software and Customer Relationship Management (CRM) software. Compiere is open source ERP software with integrated CRM solutions designed specifically for small to medium sized businesses.
- Project management software helps businesses organize their processes. Achievo is an open source web-based project management tool designed specifically for small to medium sized businesses.
- Groupware helps colleagues working on separated workstations collaborate on the same project by integrating electronic calendars, email, etc. Phprojekt is an open source groupware suite that allows workgroups to share information via intranet and internet.

Programming languages These are the high-level, human-readable languages programmers use to write source code. Several open source programming languages have become quite popular in recent years. Perl is a stable, cross platform programming language. Perl is becoming one of the most popular web programming language. PHP is a programming language that is mostly used for server-side applications and developing dynamic web content. Python is a portable object-oriented programming language.

5.3 Evaluating the Quality of Software

In the first part of this chapter we looked at which open source projects and products are popular within the community of developers and users of open source products. What we need to consider now is why people who have faithfully used proprietary software for years might switch to open source software. Open source products are taking over some markets, e.g. the Apache web server software is now used more than any other proprietary software. It would be easy to assume that the reason for this is that open source software is free and open. But is this really the case? Might people choose open source software because it is higher quality software? Before attempting to answer these questions, we must first consider how to evaluate the quality of a software product in general.

The quality of a product can be defined as the ability to satisfy requirements users have and have not explicitly expressed.[62] These requirements correspond to the needs of the various stakeholders considered and this implies that there is more than one way to evaluate quality.

Quality is a function of the technical and organizational processes used to produce or offer products and services. In fact, the ISO 9000 models, and in particular the most recent one Vision 2000, focus on achieving quality in processes and organization. The Total Quality Management (TQM) model focuses on the importance of processes as a fundamental aspect of quality competition as well. All of these considerations and evaluations have proven to be valid, but they were developed with reference to tangible, physical products and not knowledge products.

The unique characteristics of the software product influence the way in which quality can be evaluated and measured.[63]

Software is a digital product, i.e. is has no physical qualities and, therefore, none of the constraints that physical products have. Consequently, it is difficult to determine the quality of software using the traditional measurements developed for physical and tangible characteristics.

Software is also a service. Therefore, quality cannot be evaluated by only considering the quality of the product, but rather by considering the quality of the service as well.

This complexity leads to essentially two types of difficulties when evaluating software. The first type regards the fact that judgements can be subjective. Software evaluations are often based on user feedback. Software users are a very heterogeneous group of people and some of the imperfections users find might not necessarily actually be imperfections or be considered irrelevant by a part of the users. The second type of difficulty regards the need to evaluate the quality of a given software product over a long period of time so that the measurements used actually mean something. These difficulties mean that it is not easy to identify the best strategies to improve the quality of software.[64]

Theoretically, the quality of software can be evaluated by considering the number of errors or imperfections in the code. Errors can be classified according to the moment in which they became a part of the product. In other words, there are errors of analysis, design and programming. Improving the quality of the software means reducing the number of these imperfections to a minimum. Nonetheless, it is not always easy to determine what improvements need to be made because it is difficult to define rigorous quality benchmarks.

In fact, the quality of software is actually evaluated by considering not the product but the process.[65] Because software is a knowledge product, there are high product development costs and very low reproduction costs. Software is a digital product and as such in order to reproduce it all one has to do is simply copy the code. The production process of reproducing software does not in any way influence the quality of the final product. What does influence the quality of software is the development process that creates the first copy. In the next section, we will take a closer look at a model developed to evaluate the quality of software development processes, the Capability Maturity Model.

5.4 Evaluating Software Quality: the Capability Maturity Model

As has just been explained, the quality of software depends on the quality of the development process. But what is a process? A process is a set of operations, actions and changes carried out with the aim of achieving a given result. In particular, a software process is a set of activities, methods, strategies and transformations used to develop and maintain software and the products related to it. The actual results of a process define the software process performance whereas the potential of a software process describe the results that can be obtained, i.e. the software process capability. Basically, performance refers to results already obtained and capability refers to expected results.[66]

The more a process has evolved, the more capable it is and, consequently, the more mature it is. A software development process is considered mature (software process maturity) when it is formally defined, measured, controlled and managed. Maturity implies the capability to organize and foresee the activities and results of processes. A company that plans to reach the maturity of its software development process must necessarily formalize the process. This implies the development of a company culture that makes it possible to develop, diffuse and maintain methods and procedures over time. In fact, maturity can only be reached through a continuous, gradual process of transformation and improvement of all the aspects related to software development.

An important tool that is widely used to evaluate software process maturity is the Capability Maturity Model for Software (SW – CMM) developed by the Software Engineering Institute (SEI) at Carnegie Mellon University.[67] The model is a guide to help organizations that develop software achieve total control over the processes they use for developing and maintaining their software products. The aim of the Capability Maturity Model is to evaluate and improve the maturity of processes over a long period of time (software process improvement). The model evaluates the capability the process has to achieve, the type and level of quality of the results expected and the ability of the organization to continuously and gradually increase the capability and maturity of its processes.

The CMM helps companies identify the fundamental parameters and characteristics needed to determine the efficiency of their production processes, their strong points and the possible risks. By analyzing and evaluating the maturity of the processes, the model also makes it possible to evaluate the maturity of a company and as such can be used as a certification tool.

The CMM is a framework of five stages of evolution or levels of capability or process maturity. Each maturity level precisely defines the objectives and strategies needed to improve the development process. Each level adds a new characteristic to the software process until complete maturity is reached. The characteristic corresponds to the name of the level: initial level, repeatable level, defined level, managed level, and optimized level.[68] This division into five levels with precisely defined aims helps companies better manage the evolution and changes within their organizations.

At the initial level, the lowest level of maturity, the processes are not well defined nor are they effectively analyzed, evaluated or documented. The processes and their results are most likely not predictable or repeatable over time. The process management is based on reactions to events rather than planned actions. The lack of procedures and risk management have led some to call this level "ad hoc" as well. At this point of maturity, the quality of the processes and final products cannot be guaranteed.

In order to reach the second level of maturity, the repeatable level, companies must create policies and procedures to manage the software processes for larger and more complex projects. At this level, companies are forced to begin considering organizational and management problems and they must work towards becoming a learning organization, i.e. learning from the past. This level is called repeatable because the formalization of processes makes it possible to repeat the so-called "good practices". The main activities that must be carried out to manage processes are planning, scheduling, project control, and control of costs, time and quality. Problems and risks are also identified and analyzed.

At the third maturity level, the defined level, the development processes of the single projects are defined according to a standard process to which special project-specific characteristics can be added.

The aim of creating a standard process is to optimize and simplify the tasks of designing and planning each project. The documentation that describes the process must describe the policies for managing processes and the software engineering procedures. The documentation must be precise and distributed to everyone in the company. Standardization means there are the procedures and competences needed to control the main parameters that determine the quality of the processes.

A company reaches the fourth level when it has defined the measures that allow it to precisely predict and evaluate the quality of the software processes and their results. In fact, the software processes at this level are called predictable and the level managed because at this point a company is able to precisely manage and predict the quality of its processes and the products they produce. Quality and productivity measures are carried out in all the stages of the software development process and refer to a general organizational measurement program. A database, which collects and analyzes all the information, is used to develop and refine future qualitative evaluations of the processes and products.

The fifth and highest level of maturity is the optimized level. The name comes from the fact that a company that has reached this level is mature, i.e. able to predict and define the characteristics of the development processes. The aim of this level is to focus the organization's attention on the continuous improvement of the development processes. The firm must constantly develop new strategies and ideas that can help integrate technological innovation into the development processes. Costs-benefits analyses of the new technologies and changes proposed are carried out. Then the best innovations are chosen and adopted by the company. At this level a company has the tools and competences needed to improve the capability and performance of its processes in a continuous and gradual way.

To sum up, the Capability Maturity Model allows companies to understand what the level of maturity of their processes is and to identify what needs to be done to improve them. Although this model has proven to be effective in the case of commercial software, it is completely inapplicable to open source software. The lack of planning and management in the open source development process (see Chapter 3) violates all of the rules of the CMM, even the most basic ones, and would seem to indicate the incapability of the open source community to achieve high levels of quality.

The Capability Maturity Model is a descriptive model that indicates *what* must be considered to determine whether or not a process is mature and not *how* to make a process mature. It is also considered a normative model because it establishes what behaviours must be present to recognize and certify the maturity of an organization. It does not precisely define the software development process, but rather the minimum technological-organizational attributes indispensable for obtaining a high quality product.

As we have already seen, the quality of software depends mainly on the quality of the development processes. These processes are typically organized within the context of projects. In fact, the CMM exploits a series of concepts and methods typical of Project Management. It describes some levels, each of which represents an increase in complexity from the previous one and requires increasingly complex organizational capabilities to manage a software project. Nonetheless, it is also a Total Quality Management (TQM) model for organizations that develop software. As such the model includes aspects that deal with a company's technology, methods and value system. In fact, the CMM is in the same category as other models based on TQM and excellence models. In this category of models, there is an ever-increasing tendency to formalize organizational processes. This tendency makes them incapable of evaluating the development processes characteristic of the open source community. The open and unregulated nature of open source development activities does not satisfy the requirements and procedures of these models. In other words, even if the community does depend on some basic rules for behaviour, the development processes basically have not been formalized in any way.

If we were to apply the CMM to the open source development process, the apparent chaos of this process would collocate the open source process at the initial level. Since the model correlates the level of maturity to the level of quality of the product the process produces, we would have to conclude that open source products have a low level of quality. Nonetheless, there are open source products that are considered to be very high quality by users. So, the question is how does the community manage to produce high quality products? Furthermore, what new conceptual tools could be used to explain this phenomenon? The next section attempts to answer these two questions.

5.5 Evaluating Open Source Products

Users usually base their evaluation of software products on the following three main parameters:

a) reliability, i.e. the ability of the product to keep up its performance over time and in different situations;

b) performance, with particular reference to speed and features;

c) total cost of ownership, i.e. purchase and upkeep costs.[69]

The reliability of a software system can be determined using various parameters that evaluate how the system functions. The most important of these parameters is the probability of break-down, which is measured using the average amount of time the system cannot be used. The second parameter used is the average amount of time needed to fix the problem and get the system up and running again. These two parameters together can be considered down-time.

Table 5.4 – Average web server downtime per hour
(Source: AG's analysis, dwheeler.com).

Down-time 2000	Apache	Microsoft	Netscape	Others
September	5.21	10.41	3.85	8.72
October	2.66	8.39	2.80	12.05
November	1.83	14.28	3.39	6.85
Average	3.23	11.03	3.35	9.21

Table 5.4 shows the results of a research study carried out in 2000 on the average amount of downtime per hour of the web servers the 100 most visited Internet sites in Switzerland run on. The table shows that the open source web server Apache has significantly less down-time than other commercial products with the exception of Netscape Navigator. Although this particular study, which lasted only 3 months, can be

subject to criticism, it does point out two issues that are worth considering.

The first issue deals with the number of people involved in the open source software development process. There is no doubt that the more programmers there are involved in a project, the greater possibilities there are to obtain a better, more reliable product. In other words, as Raymond says "given enough eyeballs, all the bugs are shallow". From this point of view, open source products have an advantage with respect to proprietary products. Secondly, if we consider this study to be indicative of the fact that Apache is effectively more reliable than other products, we can say that it confirms the quality and potential of the open source development model in terms of reliability.

Other evaluations of open source software are based on complex benchmarking analyses of performance. In 2001, the SPEC Consortium compared the GNU/Linux operating system with Windows/OS.[70] Even if the test was not able to ascertain the predominance of one product over the other in terms of performance, it did show that the open source product is competitive. The uncertainty derived from the impossibility to carry out the tests with identical hardware and software configurations. Furthermore, there may be partial or incorrect measurements.

The third important evaluation criteria is Total Cost of Ownership (TCO). If all we consider is the cost of purchase, clearly free-of-charge open source products have a clear advantage over proprietary products. However, the TCO does not consider solely the cost of purchasing a product, but rather all of the costs including those required to maintain and manage a product. The fact that proprietary products have a higher cost of purchase is also justified by the fact that assistance and support are included in the price. This is not the case with open source products. Users of open source products nonetheless require assistance and support. In fact, there are now many companies that offer these services for open source products for a fee. In order to determine the TOC, these other costs must be considered in addition to the cost of purchase.

The freedoms granted by the open source license to distribute, modify and copy the source code free the users of OSS up from the vendor dependence that is often created with proprietary products. In other words, if a user is not satisfied with the services offered by a given OSS service supplier, the user can easily contact other suppliers. This is not the case with proprietary products. Vendor dependence for the product as well as the services and updates offered is another factor that must be considered when calculating the TOC.

What users think about the quality of a product determines to what degree the product is accepted and, therefore, diffused. Diffusion in turn determines the market share of a product. Some open source products have gained significant market shares in recent years. Software products can be divided into server-side and client-side. Open source products are more diffused on the server side than on the client side. Users of products on the server side tend to be experts and give more importance to characteristics such as reliability and performance because problems on this side affect a large number of people. On the other hand, users of products on the client side generally have less expertise and require more assistance and, therefore, tend to value other product characteristics such as user-friendliness.

The server market is dominated by two main types of products: web servers and operating systems. In both cases, open source products are gaining market share and even surpassing proprietary products.

An analysis carried out by Netcraft on web servers shows that the open source solution Apache is much more widely diffused than proprietary web servers. Over time the diffusion of Apache has significantly reduced the market share of its competitors since it entered the market.

It is more difficult to determine market shares with regards to operating systems. It is not possible to precisely monitor the number of client-side users that use different operating systems. However, it is possible to evaluate which operating systems run on the web server side. In 2001, Netcraft carried out a research study that showed a trend in favour of the increasing popularity of Linux. At the time, the Linux operating system was second only to the family of Microsoft products.

A research study carried out in 2002 by IDA (Interchange of Data between Administrations, a strategic initiative of the European Commission)[71] showed that 25% of the market share of software solutions regarding the web server side was held by open source products. Nonetheless, IDA predicted that there would be a significant diffusion of open source solutions in professional applications, even on the client side of web products (e.g. browsers).

In addition to the diffusion of Apache, other open source products for the Internet are becoming quite popular. This can be seen by the diffusion of web applications developed using open source programming languages. In a survey carried out in April 2002, Netcraft found that the open source programming language PHP was used in about 37 million of the web sites analyzed. In other words, the diffusion of PHP was greater than that of the proprietary product Microsoft ASP (Active Server Pages).

The diffusion of open source products also depends on other parameters which are, at least for now, more difficult to measure and quantify. Nonetheless, seeing that they do exist, are often important for users, and offer opportunities for comparison and evaluation, they are worth considering. These parameters are:

- *portability*, i.e. the compatibility of a product with different hardware and software systems;
- *security*, i.e. a product's ability to defend itself from violations of its integrity or from being used in inappropriate ways;
- *flexibility*, i.e. a product's ability to respond to various and multiple user needs;
- *freedom*, i.e. the possibility to freely distribute a product and to avoid vendor dependence.

There is no doubt that some open source products are compatible with a wide variety of systems. The availability of source code and the freedom to modify software according to one's needs allows the development community to continuously improve the portability of its products according to user needs. In particular, portability is an important characteristic for companies. The portability of a software product allows a company to update and substitute hardware infrastructures while keeping the software components more or less unaltered. This allows companies to save costs and time that would otherwise have to be spent on training personnel how to use new software. Finally, it is important to note that portability is also related to the freedom granted by open source licenses. Without these freedoms, it would not be possible to modify and reuse software, opportunities that proprietary software does not offer.

One way to measure product security is to consider the number and impact of the damage caused by the so-called computer viruses. Open source systems are not infallible or immune to attacks. Nonetheless, although the number of virus attacks has doubled yearly since 1988, this type of problem is much less frequent in Linux environments. In fact, Okemos, an agency specialized in insurance products for computer systems, increased the insurance premium by 5-15% for clients who do not use Unix or GNU/Linux systems in their network infrastructures.

Another factor to be considered is flexibility. Once again, the freedoms open source licenses grant allow the community to adapt and configure open source products for many different needs. In traditional one-to-many software development models all of the different user needs cannot be taken into consideration. Developing a different version of a product must be justified by the possibility of economic returns.

Finally, in addition to the freedoms to distribute, modify and copy open source software granted by open source licenses, there is another type of freedom that has recently taken on increasing importance: vendor independence. Freeing up a product from one single vendor is considered to be a way to increase competition, lower prices and speed up product innovation. This freedom also decreases the risks users run of a product being taken out of production by the vendor. In this case, freedom expresses the need of users and companies to not feel that they are "hostage" to one product and its vendor.

To sum up, although it is more difficult to evaluate OSS products we can attempt to do so by carefully examining the users satisfaction statistics regarding three basic characteristics: reliability, performance and TCO. But we must also consider other parameters that contribute to users satisfaction in the case of OSS such as portability, security, flexibility and, in particular, freedom.

Chapter 6

Strategies and Business Models

The open source phenomenon has caught the attention and interest not only of the software development community but, more recently, of companies as well. The most important companies in the Information and Communication Technology (ICT) industry have started to pay attention to and, to varying degrees, become involved in the OSS phenomenon.

Why are these companies interested in open source software? If commercial companies are showing interest, is there money to be made by getting involved in the open source community? How has the increased diffusion of open source products affected or changed competition in the ICT industry? This chapter answers these questions by moving from a general analysis of the evolution of the ICT industry to a more specific look at companies making a profit off of OSS.

First we will analyze the evolution of the competition between proprietary standards and open standards with a focus on how the OSS phenomenon has influenced and can influence this competition. Then we will take a look at the role increasing returns have played in helping diffuse OSS products. The second part of the chapter focuses on the competitive choices some of the major ICT companies have made and their relationship with the open source community. Since the OSS phenomenon has also led to the development of several new business models, we will try to understand how these models work and which companies use them.

6.1 Evolution of the ICT Industry

In order to understand the role open source software can play in the ICT industry, we must first take a look at the more general evolution of the industry. In particular, two aspects that characterize this evolution are technological convergence and competition for standards. These two aspects are related because in order to make new technologies developed in different industries compatible, i.e. to create integration, the technological standards used must be the compatible.

The world of Information Technology has been characterized by a phenomenon called digital convergence, i.e. the process of combining a set of technologies that in the past were separate in order to create new applications. Sun Microsystems expresses the concept of convergence with its motto: "The Network is the Computer". This convergence is called "digital" because it is based on the fact that data and information are now produced in digital format and are, therefore, elaborated and transmitted in a digital way. In other words, technological worlds that in the past were completely separate, such as computers and communication tools, have become integrated. In this context, software has taken on greater importance from both technological and economic points of view and has become, thanks to convergence, a tool used to link previously unconnected technological worlds. As a consequence of this technological convergence, companies working in industries not directly related to software have had to take an interest in software.

The second aspect that characterizes the evolution of the ICT industry is the competition for standards. A product, an architecture or a format becomes a standard when it is recognized by an authorized body or institution, or when it becomes widely accepted within a group of users. This can take place in a "closed" or "open" way. It is considered closed when people working in different industries do not cooperate, or only cooperate within a strategic alliance, to define a proprietary standard. An example of a creating a standard in this way is the alliance between Microsoft and Intel to create the *Wintel* standard. On the contrary, a standard is created in an open way when players in different industries cooperate to create a common standard. A standard is considered open when its specifications are publicly available and continue to be available over time. Open standards may limit a company's competitiveness on standards but this does not mean that individual players cannot compete on other technological solutions within their respective industries. An example of this strategy is the Open Shared Standard philosophy that IBM sums up with its motto "cooperate on standards, compete on solutions". Using open standards can be an advantage since, at least potentially, it means the standard is independent of one single supplier and creates interoperability, i.e. the capability to communicate between and share information with different systems.

In order to analyze the competition for standards and the diffusion of open standards, first we have to understand the architecture of computers. The architecture of a computing system describes how different components and technologies have to be integrated to make a complex system. The architecture of computing systems is made up of three main levels or macro-levels, each of which is characterized by different technologies. The first level is made up of a set of technologies, e.g. integrated circuits, microprocessors, etc., that create a hardware platform for the software technologies on the other two levels. These two levels are the system level and the application level. The system level is made up of tools that function as a communication interface between the electronic platform and the application software. Operating systems, an example of system software, are an indispensable tool for making the various hardware components work.

The application level includes the whole range of programs and applications users can execute to elaborate, manage and transmit data. Application software has to interact with system software in order to carry out its functions.

If we consider the different types of architectures and prevalent standards associated with different periods in the history of computing systems, we can identify three technological eras: systems, personal computers and network eras (Figure 6.1).[72]

During the era of systems, computer manufacturers maximized their profits by developing and controlling the entire architecture of the computer. Computer architectures were vertically integrated, i.e. companies developed all of the technologies and components needed to make a complete, ready-to-use product. In this case, we speak of

Vertically Integrated Standard Architectures, or VISA. The strategy used to design, produce and distribute computers can be called a black box strategy. Every component was the property of one company, which was responsible for the entire life cycle of the computer from planning to customer assistance. In addition to being based on the vertical integration of products, the vertical strategy was also based on protecting the property rights of the technologies developed. The various architectures were exclusively proprietary and often incompatible. Companies were in competition for their own architecture to be established as a standard in order to gain a better market share.

Figure 6.2 highlights the structure of the supply-side of the market during the era of systems.

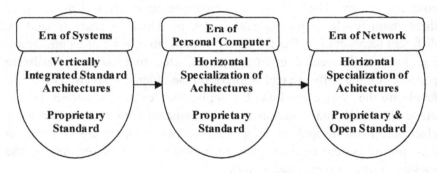

Figure 6.1 – Three technological eras.

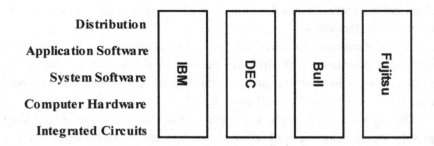

Figure 6.2 –Vertically Integrated Standard Architectures (VISA) were dominant during the era of systems (adapted from Yoffie, 1997).

In the era of systems, the dominant standard was IBM's proprietary architecture. However, IBM's vertical model was brought under question in 1969 when the United States Government brought an anti-trust suit against IBM. According to anti-trust legislation, the strong interdependency of the architecture's hardware and software thwarted competition in the industry. In response to the filing of the anti-trust suit, IBM decided to abandon its business model based on vertically integrated architecture and to sell its hardware, software and services separately. This decision meant giving up the concept of a computer built and distributed as a black box.

By abandoning the black box logic, IBM opened the way to a separation of the levels of architecture we have already mentioned. This separation allowed other companies to develop and distribute hardware, system software and application software. However, this was not enough to stimulate the emergence of other architectures that could compete with IBM's. The market continued to prefer IBM products since users considered the switching cost to other architectures to be too high. The diffusion of IBM computers did not allow other companies to exploit the economies of scale needed to support the costs of development and production. Nonetheless, the VISA strategy began to become less viable when IBM decided to turn to the help of two external companies to speed up the production and diffusion of personal computers. These companies were Intel for the supply of processors and Microsoft for operating systems. Intel and Microsoft did not have an exclusive contract with IBM and could thus sell their products to other companies as well. These changes led to the development of an industry specialized in creating products that were IBM compatible, and therefore in competition with IBM products.[73]

Competition led to the development of products that were no longer based on vertical architectures but on horizontal specialization within the individual levels of the architecture. This shift marked the end of the concept of closed architecture and the emergence of open architecture. Horizontal specialization became the dominant strategy at the same time that personal computers were becoming more and more diffused. This is why this period is called the "era of personal computers".

Distribution	Retail	Superstores	Dealers	Mail order
Application software	MS Office		WordPerfect	Altri
System Software	Dos + Windows	OS/2	Mac	Unix	Others
Computer Hardware	CompaQ	NEC	IBM	Mac	Bell	Dell
Integrated Circuits	Intel	Intel Clones	Motorola	Risc

Figure 6.3 – Horizontal specialization of architectures became dominant during the era of personal computers (adapted from Yoffie, 1997).

Open architecture produced significant changes in the competition between companies. Products belonging to different levels require different, specific competences. Consequently, companies followed a specialization strategy that led to a shift from competition based on a whole architecture to competition within each individual level (Figure 6.3).

In a vertically integrated system, the subsystems that made up one architecture, e.g. the IBM architecture, were compatible with each other but incompatible with other integrated architectures, e.g. IBM's was incompatible with DEC's. On the other hand, with a horizontal specialization strategy, the compatibility between levels guaranteed by an integrated architecture was lost and there was a greater chance of incompatibility between subsystems belonging to different levels. Therefore, the success of a component was a function of its compatibility and the possibility to integrate it with components on other levels. In other words, the more a component was compatible with other components, the more acceptable and diffused it became.[74] Strategic alliances were one way companies limited problems of incompatibility between different levels to offer users a higher quality integrated product with greater possibilities of being successful. For example, the *Wintel* alliance between *Win*dows and In*tel* allowed the two companies to take over the PC market.

While compatibility allowed companies to diffuse their products, it forced them to "loosen" their strategy of defending property rights (appropriability) and shift to a more "open" strategy. Up until this point in history, companies typically used a "closed" strategy by protecting its intellectual property and attempting to make its products become the dominant ones. The limit to this strategy is that protecting a product runs the risk of the product not being diffused. Therefore, there has to be a balance between the strategy for diffusing a product and the strategy for protecting its appropriability. An open strategy promotes product diffusion and its adoption as a standard. When an open strategy leads to the creation of a standard, it is an open standard that can be used by anyone.

The creation and diffusion of open standards are the premise for the third technological era. In this era, there is a new type of architecture that maintains horizontal specialization but takes on the characteristics of the Internet, i.e. is based on an open structure and open standards. This third evolutionary period is called the "era of the network".[75]

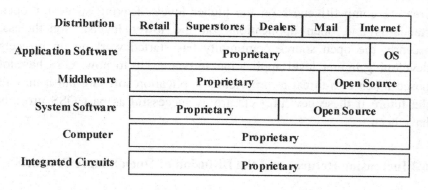

Figure 6.4 – Era of the network: open solutions.

Figure 6.4 shows the structure of the industry in the era of the network. As can be seen, there are two significant changes in this era: a new software level called middleware and the presence of open source software. The difference between the three software levels is related to how specific they are and how many applications they can support. The level of specificity increases as we move from the bottom level to the top level. On the system software level, there is not much product variety and there is a high degree of standardization. On the application level, the products are very specialized and difficult, therefore, to standardize. In other words, as we move from the lower level to the higher level, we move from standard products that are widely diffused to specific products that are generally less diffused. Middleware is the intermediate level between these two extremes. Some examples of middleware are web servers, database management systems, networking software, and application servers.

Standard products that have a low degree of specificity and a large number of users tend to be more appealing to volunteer development communities since the users are the developers of open source software. These circumstances help create the critical mass needed to efficiently develop software in the open source community. On the other hand, more specialized products with a limited number of users require specific investments and are, therefore, developed almost exclusively in proprietary contexts. Companies tend to concentrate their efforts on creating competitiveness on the higher levels, leaving space for open standards and open applications on the lower levels. Nonetheless, recently the open source community has started working on projects developing higher level application software. Up to now, OSS has not posed much of a threat to proprietary application software but it may in the future if these new projects are as successful as past OSS projects have been.

6.2 Increasing Returns and the Diffusion of Open Source Products

As we saw in the last chapter, some open source products have managed to win users over even when there are equivalent consolidated proprietary products available. However, if this is the case, how can open source products become diffused when there are existing products that are considered quasi-standards?

As was already explained in Chapter 2, software is a knowledge product and as such is governed by different economic rules than those that govern physical goods. Physical goods are "in competition", i.e. they are rival goods and cannot be used by many people at the same time.

Ideas are goods that are "not in competition", i.e. they are non-rival goods, and can be used at the same time by many people. Knowledge resources are also not as limited as physical resources. Knowledge can be used and exchanged without deteriorating. What's more, software is a digital product and can therefore be reproduced and transmitted via the Internet an infinite number of times at an irrelevant cost. The costs of developing the first copy of a new software product are very high but the copies cost almost nothing.[76]

Another important aspect of being a knowledge product is that the more a knowledge resource is used and exchanged, the more attention it attracts. The group of people who use this resource make up a network. In a network, the value of a product for a user depends on the number of other users of the same product.[77] This is called a network effect or externality. Network effects produce positive feedback which in turn helps the network grow, and as the number of members grows, the value of the network increases in an exponential way. According to Metcalfe's Law, the value of a network is proportional to the square of the number of people that the network links because this is the number of possible links. In the virtuous cycle that is created, increased network value increases the number of members in the same network because it becomes more and more interesting and advantageous to belong to that network. The network that is growing is attracting more people at the expense of other networks. This mechanism is called increasing returns, which can be defined as "[t]he tendency for that which is ahead to get farther ahead, for that which loses advantage to lose further advantage".[78]

Increasing returns lead to the creation of standards and the so-called lock-in phenomenon. A lock-in effect is created when it costs the user of a given product or technology too much to switch to a new one. There are numerous examples of lock-in in the field of technology, such as the QWERTY keyboard and the VHS system for video recording. Microsoft's MS-DOS operating system benefited from network effects and, therefore, increasing returns and lock-in effect, to become almost a standard.[79] It is important to point out that in these three cases, the products or systems were not commonly believed to be the best or highest in quality. In other words, what sometimes matters most in the creation of a standard is not necessarily quality, but rather the ability to attract a critical mass before competitors do.

Becoming a standard tends to produce monopolistic situations where an increase in prices is not the only negative effect. Another problem is the influence of monopolies on innovation. In this case, innovation is created in an essentially closed system where there is no competition. The monopoly defends the standard and its intellectual property slowing down and limiting the process of innovation. On the contrary, in an open system there is more competition and this stimulates innovation. This happens because intellectual property is open to the public, as is the case of open source software.

At the beginning of this section we posed the question, how can open source products take hold when there are existing products that are quasi-standards. The answer to this question is that not only are these products free of charge and not only is the source code available, but users believe that open source products are quality products. The lock-in effect described above depends only on network effects, and, therefore, on the value of the network. Network effects allow products that are not necessarily the best ones to become quasi-standards. In the case of open source software, we can speak of a different type of lock-in based on "product effects". The number of users and size of the network count less and the value attributed to the product more. At least for now, users who switch to open source products do so because they perceive quality in these products and not because they want or need to become part of a network of OSS users. Clearly, the low or zero cost of open source software makes it appealing, but without product quality we wouldn't be witnessing the significant switch from proprietary to open source products that has taken place, for example, with the Apache web server. In this case, there is a lock-in effect based on product quality and open source code. For the users of this type of product, the possibility to access the source code is particularly important. In other words, it is the very founding principle of the open source community, i.e. openness, that creates a lock-in. As open source application software becomes more diffused, this sort of lock-in might become more and more widespread.

6.3 Company Strategy Towards Open Source Software

The slow but ever-increasing diffusion of open source software has led commercial ICT companies to adjust their strategies to the presence of this new phenomenon. One of the most important aspects that a company must consider when defining its business strategy is how to manage intellectual property rights (IPR). IPR strategies deal with the openness and accessibility of a technology or standard with respect to customers, partners and competitors. There are different strategies ranging from a completely proprietary to an open management of property rights. It is worth asking, as Shapiro and Varian (1998) have suggested, whether it is more advantageous to focus solely on defending property rights or to have a more open strategy.

Exercising control by protecting intellectual property rights increases the unit price of products, but it can also have the effect of limiting their diffusion thus reducing the number of products sold. On the other hand, openness creates fewer obstacles to the use of a product stimulating the diffusion of the product. The value of a product for the user is greater if there are fewer limitations on the use of the product. Therefore, the problem involves finding the right balance between a strategy based on protecting intellectual property rights and one that allows users more freedoms. Basically, the aim of protecting intellectual property rights must be to maximize the value of the property. Value is maximized when there is positive feedback that makes it possible to both diffuse products and new technologies and maintain a certain degree of control over them in order to maintain an acceptable level of profit.

Many different strategies have tried to find this balance. For example, one strategy involves dividing a product into several parts and using a different approach to property rights for each part. In this way it is possible to defend the rights of some parts and, at the same time, consider other parts open. Another strategy is to offer similar, but not identical, versions of the same product. In this case, versions that are less technologically advanced or incomplete can be released for free while maintaining control over higher-quality, complete versions.

Shapiro and Varian's study deals with information goods in general and is limited to a concept of openness as access to use the good.

However, the concept of openness in the case of software is a bit more complex. In addition to the rights to access and use, in the case of software the freedom to reproduce, modify and distribute products is an issue as well. For example, where Microsoft only allows users to use the product, the open source community gives users access to the source code and, therefore, the possibility to not only use but also reproduce, modify and distribute its products.

In order to better understand what strategies are actually being adopted by major firms, we will consider three in particular: Microsoft, IBM and Sun Microsystems. Microsoft's strategy can be called a proprietary strategy, IBM's is characterized by the company's motto "cooperate on standards, compete on solutions" and Sun's can be considered a hybrid strategy involving a mixture of both proprietary and open source solutions.

A proprietary strategy is a closed strategy that uses copyright and patents to exercise complete control of information. This means that access to information is only permitted in one big block following the purchase of a product. This is the case of Microsoft.

Microsoft considers the software that is developed and distributed in the open source community to be a valid alternative to its proprietary strategy and, therefore, to be a potential threat to profits in the short run and as a development model in the long run. Microsoft recognizes the fact that open source software has achieved a maturity and complexity comparable, if not superior, to those that characterize products developed using more commercial development models.

In reaction to the threat posed by open source software, Microsoft set up the Shared Source project. This initiative is Microsoft's attempt to learn about and transfer aspects of the open source model to its own development model. Shared Source is a sort of compromise between the advantages that can be gained by a partial opening of its source codes and defending its intellectual capital at the same time. The Shared Source strategy, by protecting property rights, limits the free distribution and sharing of software and source codes. It is a *read-only* strategy that allows those who have a Shared Source contract to read the code but not to modify or correct it. The numerous restrictions that characterize these contracts continue to prevent Microsoft from achieving an extensive and complete peer review of its source codes.

Though the Shared Source project may give the impression that Microsoft is opening up some of its code, the project is actually not compatible with the concepts and philosophy open source development is based on. Shared Source can be seen as a reaction to the open source model and an attempt to limit the diffusion of open source products, licenses and development model. Bruce Perens claims that Shared Source confuses ideas: "Microsoft's Shared Source program recognizes that there are many benefits to the openness, community involvement, and innovation of the Open Source model. But the most important component of that model, the one that makes all of the others work, is freedom. By attacking the one license that is specifically designed to fend off their customer and developer lock-in strategy, they hope to get the benefits of Free Software without sharing those benefits with those who participate in creating them."[80]

Whereas Microsoft is mainly a software company, IBM has decided that the most interesting and profitable market today for an ICT company is not the product market but rather the services market, e.g. offering training, consulting and support. In recent years IBM has recognized that significant profits can be made by selling not only systems with proprietary software but systems with open source software as well. The company's strategy can be defined as competitive cooperation, where competition on services is favoured by cooperating on technologies and infrastructures.

IBM recognizes the value and opportunities offered by the open source model for its strategy of competitive cooperation. IBM's initiative Open Shared Standard is aimed at the development of freely accessible open standards. This initiative can be justified by the need to develop standard products able to guarantee a free and competitive market for IBM's future applications. An open standard also guarantees greater product flexibility and quality. The initiative basically uses the open source model to promote innovation, integration and the collaborative development of standards that can benefit the entire industry. As the former president of IBM Italy, Elio Catania, explains: "The difference is that Microsoft still doesn't understand that money will be made less and less on software and more and more on services. [...] they [Microsoft] aim at privatizing and having a monopoly on public services (i.e. technological standards), we [IBM] prefer that our systems work as an open infrastructure, able to guarantee interoperability between different products, and we plan on making money by selling services one level above the infrastructure level."[81]

Sun Microsystems is another major company in the ICT market that has realized the growing importance of open source software in the ICT market. Sun's strategy is based on open-sourcing its commercial products and directly participating in developing the open source versions and, vice versa, integrating open source software in its proprietary solutions. Sun, which stands for Stanford University Network, is a company that has its roots in a university environment close to the concepts of openness and freedom. In fact, the first microcomputers the company distributed were powered by the BSD operating system, which was free, open software. These origins have influenced Sun's continuous involvement in the open source development community. In 1984, Sun introduced its network file sharing technology and licensed it for free. This technology subsequently became the industry standard for network file sharing. In 1995, Sun introduced Java, an object-oriented programming language that could be considered a universal software program designed for the Internet and intranets. Applications written in Java can run on any computer making Java the main programming language of the Internet. In February 2004, in an open letter to Sun, Eric Raymond called on Sun to open source Java, and later the same year, Sun announced that the company was planning to do just that, without specifying when it would happen.[82] In 1999, Sun entered the Desktop market by acquiring the StarOffice suite of software from a German company. It released StarOffice 5.2 in June, 2000 and at the end of the same year released the source code for StarOffice under the GNU General Public License launching an open source office suite software project called OpenOffice.org. Subsequent versions of StarOffice, beginning with 6.0, have been built using much of the technology created by OpenOffice.org. In 2004, Sun also announced plans to open source another one of its major products: the Solaris operating system. Sun's intention seems to be to compete with the Linux operating system. The company is very much involved in and sponsors other open source projects as well, such as Mozilla (web browser) and GNOME (desktop suite and development platform). Sun's Java Desktop System (second release in May 2004) includes a mixture of its own commercial products (StarOffice, Java) and open source products (Mozilla, GNOME). To sum up, Sun's strategy is quite complex and could even be considered a sort of a laboratory of how companies can be involved in open source projects and mix open source solutions with their own commercial products. In fact, as will be seen in the next section, Sun's strategy can even be considered a new business model based on open source software.

6.4 Can Open Source Software Lead to New Business Models?

Open source software has not only affected the strategies of major ICT companies, but it has also influenced the business models of small and start-up ICT firms. The recent increase in the number of smaller companies that base their business in some way on open source products leads to questions that must be answered. Since open source software products are basically free, how can smaller and start-up companies make money with open source software? Is it possible to build a business around open source software?

In order to answer these questions and understand the relationship between business and open source software, we must first understand that the software business does not involve only development. We can divide the software value chain into two groups of activities: production/programming and services. The main activities in the production part are development, documentation and packaging. For the service part they are consulting, implementation and integration, training and support and application management.

There are two different models for the software value chain: one-to-many or one-to-one. When most people think of software, they think of one-to-many products, i.e. major commercial software such as Microsoft Office. However, the amount of code that is written for sale is only a very small part of the code that is written. Most software is actually written in-house by external software companies for the specific needs of banks, businesses, hospitals, etc. Although the order in which all of the activities are carried out in the two models may vary, what they do have in common is the important role services play.

Whereas in traditional industries, a large part of a product's value chain centres around development and production, in the case of software these activities occupy only a small part of the value chain. According to Eric Raymond, "...software is largely a service industry operating under the persistent but unfounded delusion that it is a manufacturing industry".[83] Over two-thirds of a software's life-cycle costs involve the activities in the services part of the value chain, e.g. de-bugging, updating, customizing, etc. In fact, software engineers dedicate more of their time to maintenance than to developing or programming. In other words, the software business is a new kind of business which is greatly based on services.

The new business models that have been created around open source software are, in fact, based on services. In the more traditional model of proprietary software, profit comes from the sale of licenses. The license defines who can use the software and states that the software is the intellectual property of the company that is supplying it. Services such as implementation, training and debugging are included in many of these licenses. In the case of open source software the open source license is free. Although the software can be downloaded, used and redistributed for free, technical support is a part of this free package. If we put aside the few exceptions of university departments or companies that have specialized technicians who do not require technical support, what is lacking in the open source model is the entire services part of the value chain. The new business models take advantage of this: revenue is generated not from licensing fees but by selling services.

The new business models can be divided into two general categories. The first category is made up of companies that create services around products that have already been developed by the open source community. The second category is made up of companies that offer services around their own proprietary products that they have opened up, or vice versa, for which a proprietary version has been made. Given that we are dealing with open source software that has been developed by the community of volunteer programmers, in all the models revenue comes from services and not development.

Table 6.1 – New business models based on OSS.

	Business Model	Example
Create new business off of open source software	Competence-based services	Linux Care
	Distribution, services and branding	Red Hat
	Widget frosting	Dell, IBM
	Accessorizing	O'Reilly
Create new software and follow a hybrid approach	Loss leader	Mozilla
	Free the software, sell the brand	OpenOffice.org
	Dual licensing	MySql
	Dual mission	Sendmail

As can be seen in Table 6.1, there are four models in the first category: competence-based services, distribution, services and branding, widget frosting and accessorizing. In the first model, competence-based services, a company works as a paid consultant offering services on the basis of the expert competences of its employees. An example of this model is LinuxCare, a firm that sells support for GNU/Linux systems. The firm was born in 1998 out of the need to offer assistance to the growing community of Linux users. LinuxCare has set up partnerships with many major hardware and technology companies such as HP, IBM, Fujitsu, Siemens, etc. LinuxCare offers its partners a series of services to choose from to meet the needs of their customers. In this way, the hardware company can install open source software on its machines without having to be responsible for the implementation and maintenance of the software. The license LinuxCare uses is the GPL. The company tries to attract the most talented software engineers in the industry who are experts in open source software. The open source code allows these engineers to customize the software, integrate it with other systems, make modifications and meet all the needs of the clients. The critical success factors of this model are the high level of knowledge of the employees and the fact that the company maintains a relationship with the open source development community.

The distribution, services and branding model goes one step beyond the first model by offering a brand. One way of describing this model is that it is an attempt to offer more or less what proprietary software offers: certification, a reliable brand, warranties and support. In this model, a company takes open source software, e.g. Linux, creates a tested user-friendly package around it and offers support. In this model, the company offers its version of an open source product and generates revenue by selling two broad categories of items: physical goods, e.g. hard-copy documentation, and/or services, e.g. training, consulting, customizing and technical support. Probably the most successful example of a company that uses this model is Red Hat. Red Hat was the first company to offer this sort of service and its distribution has had such a success that many people identify Linux with the Red Had brand. Robert Young, co-founder of Red Hat, states that the company operates "...much like a car assembly plant—[they] test the finished product and offer support and services for the users of the Red Hat Linux OS".[84] Red Hat also has a strong commitment to supporting the open source development community. It founded the Red Hat Advanced Development Labs and employs skilled programmers to work on developing open source software. This way the company can develop an improved version of their own brand-named product and at the same time collaborate to develop new open source software. The critical success factors of this model are the brand, service, free distribution and involvement in the open source community.

Widget frosting has become a term that is by now well-known in the software the ICT industry. In this model companies that mainly sell hardware ("widgets") use open source software ("frosting") either because it can be distributed at no cost along with the hardware or because it makes the hardware more functional, reliable and useful. "Frosting" their products with open source software costs these hardware manufacturers nothing. In some cases, it can give them an economic advantage by charging their customers less. In other cases, giving customers access to source code and, therefore, the ability to modify it as needed can guarantee customers come back to the same company when the production and support life-cycle of the hardware is over. There are many well-known companies that use this model such as Dell Computers and IBM, both of which offer customers the option to buy standard PC hardware with Microsoft Windows or Linux. This model offers hardware manufacturers the possibility to widen their customer base.

The last model in our first category is the accessorizing model. As the name itself indicates, in this model a company sells accessories for open source software. These accessories can range from anything like Linux penguin dolls to reference volumes on open source software. In other words, a company distributes physical items associated with and supportive of open source software but does not actively participate in the development of open source software. A well-known example of a company that uses this model is the book publisher O'Reilly & Associates. Not only does this company publish hard-copy versions of its books on open source software, but it also offers the contents of some books for free online. By publishing books explaining open source products, this company has also managed to create some brand loyalty among people who use and support open source software.

With the loss leader model, businesses are willing to lose money in order to become a leader in the market in the future. In the case of software, a proprietary software company decides to become involved in an open source project or develop open source products in order to create or maintain its market position for proprietary software. This is the model Netscape used in 1998 when it decided to open source its browser Netscape Navigator and create the open source version of it called Mozilla. Microsoft's browser Internet Explorer was taking market share away from Netscape Navigator and gaining a monopoly. The Mozilla project led to a collaboration with the open source community that not only created the Mozilla browser but helped Netscape improve and fix the bugs in its proprietary Navigator browser as well.

The "free the software, sell the brand" model can be seen as the loss leader model repeated over time. A commercial software company starts out its products' life-cycles by selling them as proprietary products but then opens them up at a certain point. This point is reached when the benefits of developing the products in collaboration with the open source community are greater than the revenue that can be gained from selling licenses.

The company can then sell services, hardware, etc. around the product it has open-sourced and use the collaboration to improve the commercial version of the product. Furthermore, the open source product helps sell the brand for the company's commercial products as well. For example, Sun Microsystems spent years developing and selling its commercial office suite StarOffice and then opened up the code to the open source community creating the open source version OpenOffice.org. Sun Microsystems also sells its brand by reminding OpenOffice.org users of its sponsorship of the project by including the company name and logo on all of the pages in the OpenOffice.org website.

Another business model that involves open sourcing a commercial product is the dual licensing model. The difference here is that the same product is sold with a commercial license and offered under an open source license as well. These companies make their revenue by selling the commercial software licenses and services and support for users with either type of license. This model allows companies to offer customers a choice. Customers who are particularly interested in or faithful to open software and the open philosophy can get the open source version. On the other hand, those who want the packaging, documentation and support characteristic of commercial software can buy the proprietary product. In particular, this model allows the company to have a paid development team dedicated to one particular product. This guarantees consistency in upgrades, and professional documentation and support. Furthermore, customers can be sure that the vendor has full rights to the intellectual property in the software. Finally, it offers the benefits from opening code up to the open source community that are also achieved in the previous two models, i.e. free help from a community of software developers in improving code and fixing bugs, freedom from vendor lock-in, faster time-to market. The most successful example of this model is MySql. MySql is the most popular open source database in the world and is used by The Associated Press, Google and NASA.

The last model is in many ways the opposite of the models proposed so far, i.e. it involves "closing" or making commercial versions of originally open products. This model is very unique because it can only be applied once an open product has become widely diffused. It can be used by companies whose original mission was to promote innovation and reliability with open source software. The motivations behind closing a product are similar to those behind the dual licensing model. In both models two versions of the same product are offered. The reason for offering a commercial version is that it satisfies the needs of some customers to have commercial packages, service and support. Sendmail Inc. is an example of a hybrid company with a dual mission. Sendmail, the dominant mail transfer technology on the Internet, was developed at the University of Berkeley at the beginning of the eighties as a product free of any intellectual property rights. After nearly 20 years of being a freeware product, in 1998 Sendmail Inc. was founded to offer cost-effective commercial packages of Sendmail. At the same time, the open source community continues to develop new releases of the open source version of Sendmail.

It should be clear that although OSS does not pose a serious threat to commercial software it is clearly influencing the strategies of both established and new firm. In the next chapter we will see how it is also influencing the major choices regarding IT made by governments around the world.

Chapter 7

Government Policies Towards
Open Source Software

As we saw in the last chapter, there is a growing interest in the open source phenomenon outside the community itself. Not only have companies begun to become interested in open source software, but governments around the world have as well. The choices governments make regarding ICT have a widespread influence on society. First of all, they spend very large amounts of money annually on ICT. Secondly, the public in general, users of public services, have a direct relationship with governments. Consequently, the choices governments make have an impact on the choices its citizens will then make in their personal lives.

This chapter begins with a general discussion of the factors in favour of governments adopting open source software and the limiting factors involved as well. Then we will see what four scholars think the role of governments in supporting and/or adopting open source software should be. Finally, we will take a look at what open source software policies governments around the world have actually been developing.

7.1 Factors in Favour of Governments Adopting Open Source Software

The ICT needs of governments are different from those of companies and individual users. Therefore, before considering what they might gain by adopting open source software, we must first understand what specific needs they have. These needs can be divided into two general categories: economic needs and information management needs.

As far as the economic needs are concerned, obviously governments, like companies, need to reduce or at least contain ICT costs as much as possible. However, governments, not companies, are most likely the largest coordinated buyers of software in the world. Given the large size of governments, public administrations and other public offices, for example, just paying the software licensing fees for commercial software can be a significant cost. In addition to this cost, governments also often have to customize software to meet their specific needs. Customizing commercial software is costly both because the organization has to pay the supplier of the software to carry out the customization and because it must then pay additional fees to re-use and diffuse the customized software. Since different local governments must exchange information both with each other and with the central government, the software used to exchange and process data should be the same or at least compatible. In this context, the possibility to diffuse and re-use software becomes very important.

The other category of needs deals with the fact that governments have to exchange data with the public, and process and store private information regarding citizens. One of the primary needs of governments is to have software that can guarantee the security and privacy of information. Furthermore, governments must guarantee the public access to information and make sure information be exchanged easily regardless of the technology used. Finally, they have to guarantee information be accessible in the long run even if a given software becomes obsolete.

Table 7.1 shows what the needs of public administrations are and how open source software and open formats and standards can satisfy them.

The initial costs of adopting open source software can allow governments to save money in terms of not having to buy licenses. The cost of updating commercial software should also not be undervalued since major updates mean buying new licenses for all users. However, the overall cost of software is not made up only of licensing fees.

The Total Cost of Ownership (TCO) does not consider solely the cost of purchasing a software license, but what maintenance, upgrades, technical support and training cost as well. The TCO must be evaluated by considering the entire life cycle of a product. In the case of switching from commercial software to open source software, the TCO includes the costs of migration, installation, training, support and management.

Table 7.1 – Government ICT needs and how open source software and open standards can meet these needs.

Type of need	Need	How open source software and open standards can meet the need
Economic factors	Reduce ICT costs	There are no licensing fees and customizing costs are reduced because the source code is available.
	Transfer modified software to other government bodies	Open source software can be re-used and diffused.
Information management and public relations	Guarantee security and privacy	Source code availability makes it possible to check the source code and modify it if necessary.
	Guarantee public access to information regardless of technology used	Independence from vendors
	Guarantee information exchange be easy and effective	Interoperability
	Guarantee possibility to access information in the long run	Technological continuity

Therefore, it is important to thoroughly evaluate the relationship, in the long run, between the benefits and overall costs of using and maintaining the software. Though the costs of switching might be significant, an argument in favour of using open source software is that the money saved on licenses could be spent on services which would lead to improved services from a qualitative point of view. By not being dependent on one vendor, governments adopting open source software have more options in choosing the best offer for services, maintenance and support. Though the TCO of using open source software might not be less than the TCO of using commercial software, the open source solution offers greater flexibility in deciding how and where to spend the money in the budget.

Access to the source code gives governments the possibility to customize software to meet their specific needs. These organizations often have technicians able to do this and don't necessarily have to pay external consultants to do it for them. What's more, once the software has been modified, it not only has to be installed on all of the workstations in that particular organization, but it often has to be shared with other local or central government offices as well. All open source licenses make re-use and distribution possible. A GPL license, for example, allows users to re-use and diffuse software without ever having to pay for licenses.

The advantages of using open source software are not only economic. In fact, many of the arguments in favour of using open source software in pubic administrations are technical. Commercial tools may not necessarily guarantee the security that public administrations require for transmitting information to citizens. In order to guarantee security and confidentiality, technicians within the pubic administration must have access to the source code in order to close any "back doors", i.e. weak points that make the software susceptible to outside attacks. In the case of commercial software, where there is no access to the source code, only the vendor can provide this service. Open source code allows public administrations to verify that the software meets all its security needs and adapt if it doesn't. With access to the source code technicians can isolate and fix bugs or adapt the software to meet new needs.

One of the main benefits of using open source software is the commitment the community has to developing software that is interoperable and respects open standards. Whereas commercial companies use commercial standards to protect their captive market, the open source community wants to keep standards public and common because it believes that it is in the best interest of everyone to do so. Citizens have the right to easily access information and it is the duty of public administrations to guarantee the public accessibility. Each person should be able to access information and documents regarding them without having to use a specific software product. This can only happen if data is archived using platforms, protocols and formats that are based on open standards. In other words, using open formats makes vendor independence possible.

Another benefit of open standards is that they offer interoperability. As we have already said, information exchange is one of the main responsibilities of governments, making interoperability a fundamental pre-requisite.

Finally, open source software has no commercial owner and, therefore, no one can stop or "kill" the program. If companies go bankrupt or merge with other companies, users may be forced to migrate to new commercial solutions. This is particularly important for governments because information must be accessible over time. If platforms and applications change, governments are faced with the problem of not being able to guarantee the perenniality of information or guaranteeing it at significant costs. On the other hand, since open source software makes the source code available and in doing so contributes to the development of open standards, open source software makes it easier to guarantee information be readily accessible in the long-run. Considering the amount of information stored in electronic format today and the rate at which technology changes, technological continuity is of fundamental importance for governments.

7.2 Limiting Factors for the Adoption of Open Source Software

We have seen that using open source software could offer governments many advantages, but what are the drawbacks or limiting factors? For each of the advantages mentioned above, there may also be a disadvantage or problem that must still be solved. In Table 7.2, the advantages and relative limiting factors of using open source software in governments are summarized.

Although no licensing fees have to be paid to use open source software, a migration from commercial software to open source software, especially considering the large number of users in government offices, can be significant. For example, staff have to be trained to use the new software, information must be converted to be accessible and used in the new system and technicians may have to learn to carry out some of the assistance that was previously offered by the commercial software vendor. In other words, it's not just a simple issue of licensing costs.

There is no question that open source code offers open source software users the possibility to modify software to meet their needs and reuse it. Furthermore, the licenses that accompany open source software make it possible to widely diffuse the software used. These are certainly advantages of open source software, but only once it is being used.

Table 7.2 – Advantages and limitations of adopting open source software.

Advantages	Limitations
Reduced cost	Migration costs
Reuse and diffusion	Limited number of existing open source application programs
Interoperability (open standards)	Lack of Interoperability open source software -commercial software
Independence from vendors	Existing long-term contracts Lack of accountability Risk of software patent liability
Perenniality	Longevity of existing commercial systems

At present, there is a limited number of pre-existing open source application programs and the number of commercial applications that can run on open source operating systems is small compared to those available for commercial ones. In fact, the open source community has focused its efforts on collective needs and mass projects rather than on specialized applications. Though this may change in the future, currently there are no specific open source software application programs for governments.

Open standards make interoperability a point in favour of open source software for users who use only open source software. However, the fact is that most government offices currently use commercial software. A switch from this software to open source software would certainly not be immediate, but rather gradual. For a certain period of time governments would have to be using both types of software and the interoperability between the two is currently not guaranteed. Exchanging documents between different applications requires conversions. Filters must be able to convert all of the information in complex documents in order to avoid losing information. However, currently open source office solutions have not been able to achieve 100% interoperability with the dominant Microsoft Office suite for documents that have a complex structure. In other words, sharing files can be difficult, if not impossible at times. There are also interoperability problems on the hardware level. The operating system must be able to communicate with the drivers that control hardware devices such as printers, monitors, scanners, etc. Many hardware manufacturers still do not sell their products with drivers for Linux. Although the open source community is aware of this problem and has been developing drivers, not all drivers are supported in all installations.

Independence from vendors may give public administrations more flexibility in modifying the software to meet their needs and increased possibilities to ensure information security. However, it may also have some drawbacks. First of all, many public administrations are currently bound by existing long-term contracts with large ICT companies that must be respected. Secondly, there may be a certain lack of accountability in the case of open source software since the community itself, which does not sell the software, cannot be held legally responsible for any problems or difficulties with the software it develops. This problem is becoming less significant as the number of open source software distributors and hardware vendors that integrate open source software grows. These companies offer support and maintenance contracts that guarantee assistance be given when needed. Although the community can offer free support, this support is unpredictable and no one will accept liability for it. In the unstable ICT market, large commercial software firms might be able to guarantee more consolidated support over time than the new open source software distribution companies. Nonetheless, this too remains to be seen since some of these new companies, such as Mandrake, SuSe/Novell and Red Hat, are becoming more and more reliable. Finally, there is the problem of software patents. As has already been explained in Chapter 2, open source software is at risk as software patents become more and more used both in the United States and in other countries. For example, since the source code is open, a commercial software company could potentially put a patent on an algorithm developed by the open source community and implemented in open source software. If this were to happen, then the company that deposits the patent could make open source software users pay a fee to use the open source software containing the newly patented algorithm. This could potentially be detrimental in the case of large scale use of open source software in governments.

As we have already pointed out, the fact that open source software has no commercial owner, means that no one can stop or "kill" the program. Though this may guarantee perenniality for open source software, the longevity of other commercial systems, e.g. Microsoft Windows and Unix, cannot be disputed. For years these products have offered users a single commercial road map to meet most of their needs.

7.3 What Role Should Governments Play in Supporting and/or Adopting Open Source Software?

The choices governments make to support and/or adopt open source software could have a widespread effect on the choices the public makes and, therefore, the role of governments potentially influences the market. For example, by using open source software, European governments could help promote the ICT industry in Europe. This industry in Europe has not been able to keep up with the developments of the ICT industry in the United States and Asia. Many European information technology companies have left the market. Open source software could be the opportunity to gain ground and support the development of a new ICT industry based on services for open source software in which Europe could play a fundamental role.

Industries cannot, however, go it alone. Governments could also play a role. What exactly should the role of governments be? Should they be actively involved in promoting open source software or leave it up to the market to decide whether commercial or open source software is the best solution? When the market mechanism works, it offers customers the best product available. When they do not work there are "market failures", which means that products can become widely diffused and accepted even if they do not offer enough user satisfaction or are not the best solution possible. In this case, the inadequate selection of the market could justify an intervention on the part of public institutions. It is worth asking, then, if this type of public intervention can be justified in the case of software. To try and answer this question we will take a look at the different points of view of James Bessen, David Evans, Bradford Smith and Lawrence Lessig.[85]

Bessen does not consider open source software to be an alternative to traditional software, but rather sees it as complementary to the qualities and characteristics that commercial software offers.[86] He does not identify any actual market failures in software, but believes open source software can offer the opportunity to overcome some of the imperfections and contractual constraints of commercial software. In other words, he maintains that the two models should co-exist. Governments should not favour one solution over another but rather make a careful comparison of the two based on an analysis of the costs and benefits. One of the elements to be considered when making this analysis is the ability to continually modify the product. In this case, open source software offers greater flexibility than commercial software. Another factor to consider is the possibility of a lock-in phenomenon (see Chapter 6). Adopting open source software could help free the software market up from lock-in phenomena and stimulate competitiveness in the software industry. Nonetheless, Bessen does not believe governments should play a role in financially supporting the development of open source products. The diffusion and growth of open source software has taken place up to now without public intervention. He does maintain, though, that governments could intervene on a legal level in order to limit the negative effects of current laws regarding patents and property rights.

Evans, in agreement with Bessen, is convinced that there has not been any real market failure in the software industry. He believes that governments should not directly support open source software or commercial software. However, he does recognize the efficiency of the open source software development model, which is based on cooperation, and the validity of alternative ways of organizing software development. Evans maintains that the development of software in a public environment can take place using open source methods but that there should also be the possibility for the results of these activities to be further developed by private companies. According to Evans, this possibility is limited by open source licenses. In particular, he criticizes the GPL license because it is too restrictive for companies. Therefore, he argues that other open source licenses must be used in order to get companies interested and involved.[87]

Smith agrees with Evans and Bessen that there has been no market failure in the software market. He also points out that the initiatives of some large companies highlight the fruitful integration of open source software and commercial software. He believes that governments should not intervene on the market, but that if they do, these interventions could have significant effects on the software market. Finally, he argues that if they participate in developing open source software, this intervention should not limit the possibility to commercialize the results.[88]

Lessig's views on market failure are different from the three opinions we have considered so far. He claims that there could be market failure for open source software. Open source software developers might be demotivated by the impossibility of receiving financial compensation for their work on open source projects. This could limit interest in open source projects with consequences on product quality and performance. Nonetheless, Lessig recognizes the fact that there are other factors that motivate open source programmers and have helped the community of independent volunteers grow and develop quality products.

Lessig agrees with the others that governments should maintain as neutral a position as possible and consider economic factors when choosing what software to use. However, he argues that governments should take a more decisive stance regarding the development and diffusion of open standards. Furthermore, he maintains that open source licenses, including the GPL, are valid and should be used by governments.

To sum up, there seems to be significant agreement on the fact that both commercial and open source software are important and that they should co-exist. All four scholars agree that governments should not become excessively involved in directly supporting or developing open source software. This is what four important scholars in the field think about the role of governments, but what are governments actually doing? In the next section we will take a look at the open source software polices governments in various countries around the world have been developing and implementing.

7.4 Government Policies Toward Open Source Software in Various Countries

In many countries around the world, governments have started initiatives that directly or indirectly promote the use of open source software. In 1999, one year after the Open Source Initiative was founded, some countries began evaluating open source software. This phenomenon started in Europe. Five years after these initiatives were first launched, the European Union began to officially consider using open source software and developed instructions to help guide member countries in making decisions regarding open source software. Today the policies of the different member countries still vary quite a bit. Particular interest seems to be coming from local governments, especially in big cities (e.g. Paris, Munich, Rome). Nonetheless, even within this group there are significant differences in policy, ranging from those that are openly in favour of adopting open source software to those which are more conservative. Quite often these differences of opinion exist not only between countries, but between local administrations as well. In other words, the degree to which governments are convinced that open source software offers interesting solutions still varies significantly.

An analysis of the open source software policies of various governments indicates that, in general, the switch from using solely commercial software to using open source software usually takes place in three steps. First the government carries out a study on the potential benefits of adopting open source software. Then, based on results the study, or studies, the government develops its policy on open source software. The policy may simply involve offering advice or writing norms regarding the adoption of open source software. The third step is implementation. However, it is important to point out that in many cases initiatives on a local level either took place in parallel with initiatives on a national level, or, in some cases, were the stimulus for central governments to carry out the studies.

Before beginning our description, it should be pointed out that the information contained in this section is in continuous evolution. Therefore, this section can be considered a panorama of what has taken place to date and what some possible courses of action are for governments and governmental policy.

7.4.1 European countries

France and Germany are currently the two countries in Europe that have been most active in developing concrete initiatives in the field of open source software on the national and local levels. Other countries that have also developed open source policies are the United Kingdom, Italy, Spain, Austria, Belgium, Sweden, Ireland and Finland. Though not part of the EU, the policies in Norway and Russia are closely related to those developed in the EU countries.

Germany. Germany has played a major role in Europe in developing government policy toward open source software. There have been initiatives at all levels of government, from the Federal Government down to local governments. On a national level, the Federal Government maintains that open source software can help in the development of an information society and has started a series of initiatives aimed at better understanding the advantages and disadvantages of adopting open source software. In 2000, the Government set up a national centre for open source competences in order to provide the necessary technical infrastructures to support open source research, development, and discussions. In particular, the Government was interested in the involvement of the open source community with regards to improving the security of data processing and data communications. In 2000, the Federal Ministry of Economic Affairs published a guide to information technologies and communication within the Federal Administration. The guide lays out what the advantages of open source software are, how it can be integrated with commercial software and how migration from commercial to open source software can be carried out. In the same year, the Ministry of Interior published a letter giving information and guidelines on adopting and using open source software. The Ministry of Economics and Labour, again in 2000, published an informative document regarding the use of open source software in SMEs (Small to Medium Enterprises). This same Ministry also founded and supports the BerliOS project together with FOKUS (Research institute for open communication systems). "The goal of BerliOS is to provide support for different interest groups in the area of Open Source Software. Our aim is to fulfill a neutral mediator function. The target groups of BerliOS are on one hand the developers and users of Open Source Software and on the other hand commercial manufacturers of open source software operating systems and applications as well as support companies."[89]

The Federal Government has also participated in developing open source software for government uses. Starting in December 1999, the Federal Ministry of Economics and Technology decided to financially support the implementation of an open source encryption system for electronic mail. The project was called "Open Source and IT-Security Enhancement and Marketing of GNU Privacy Guards (GnuPG)". The Federal Government has placed particular attention on the fact that open source software can offer not only lower costs, but increased security. Together with a private company in Bremen, the German Federal Ministry of the Interior developed the software Governikus, a secure middleware platform that enables secure, traceable and confidential communication between public bodies, and between them and external organizations involved in e-government services. All of the interfaces of Governikus were built using OSCI (Online Services Computer Interface), an open communications protocol for the secure transfer of documents with digital signatures. In 2003, the Ministry of the Interior announced the entire federal administration would use Governikus.

More recently, the German Government has helped financed the development of an open source desktop solution for public administrations based on Linux in order to lower costs, increase stability and security and limit the dependence on commercial products. This project helped contribute to improvements in KDE, an open source graphical desktop environment that make Linux more user-friendly. The

Linux Government Desktop, developed by the German Federal Office for Information Security together with a private company, was unveiled during LinuxTag 2004. It is composed entirely of free software, manages encrypted filesystems, can send and receive encrypted e-mail, manage digital signatures, and offers spam and virus protection.

On a local level, the case of the city of Munich is particularly important. During the first months of 2003, the city announced plans to make a gradual shift from Windows NT to the Linux operating system rather than upgrade its 14,000 desktop PCs to the latest versions of Windows and Office. Following the announcement, Microsoft lowered its price offer quite a bit two times in the hope of keeping the contract. However, on May 28, 2003, the city council approved a more expensive proposal from German Linux distributor SuSE and IBM. What is particularly noteworthy about the LiMux Project, as it is known in Germany, is the choice not only to use Linux but to use open source desktop applications, i.e. OpenOffice and Mozilla. On June 18, 2004, the city announced that the year-long trial had been a success and that the migration would officially begin on July 1, 2004. The migration would be carried out in three stages and be complete by 2008 or 2009. The city council members pointed out the importance of involving a large number of smaller companies in the project, in particular local ones, in order to help the local economy and avoid one monopolistic company being replaced by another.

However, in August 2004, concerns over software patents led the city of Munich to temporarily put the project on hold. City officials announced that they had to assess the risks patents might have on LiMux in light of software patent legislation currently under consideration in the European Parliament. The fear is that should LiMux's proposed software have conflicts with existing or future patents, a company holding the patent could effectively shut down the city's computer systems or force them to pay licensing fees. For the time being, the city has actually decided to go on with the first stage of the process and started selecting bidders. However, the mayor has stated that the future of the project might depend on the outcome of the patent controversy in Europe.

France. France has played a major role in the diffusion of open source software in Europe. The French Government considers open source software to be one of its main priorities. The French Government has considered the use of open source solutions and technologies on a national level in fields and industries regarding the environment, transportation, healthcare, technologies for the disabled and on-line training and learning. In 1998, the French Government started using open source software in some of its information systems. The Ministry of Defense adopted the FreeBSD system because it considered this software to be more reliable and secure. The Ministry of Justice and the "Casier Judiciaire National" began to use the open source products Apache, Perl, Samba and Fetchmail. And the Ministry of the Economy, Finance and Industry and the General Management of Customs approved plans to restructure their information systems with the aim of using Red Hat Linux 6.2 in its server and workstations.

In 1998, an inter-Ministry project (MTIC) was set up to develop and implement ICT projects in the Government and public administrations. The project focused on issues dealing with IT technologies, standards and interoperability. Part of the project included discussions, meetings, seminars and events regarding open source software.

In 2001, the French Agency for e-Government (ATICA) decided to start a selection process for the use of open standards in public administrations. The aim of this initiative was to improve and guarantee the technological interoperability of public functions. The Agency also has the official task of promoting the development and diffusion of open source software. Finally, it is responsible for choosing the most appropriate license for the future distribution of software developed within the Government and public administrations.

The City administration of Paris announced in February 2004 that it had decided to launch a study of the feasibility of an open source migration for all of the local government's workstations. The aim of the study is to consider the possibilities of using open source software for its PCs, servers and desktop and database applications. The City chose Unilog, the same IT services company that carried out a study for the City of Munich prior to its migration decision, to conduct the study for Paris.

At the beginning of 2004, the French Government announced it was planning to migrate to open source software for a large number of the

Government's 900,000 desktop computers. The migration would be part of the larger project ADELE (ADministration ELEctronique). The main aim of ADELE is to connect all public agencies, central to local governments and public-services agencies, within a single electronic infrastructure. The project would include a series of smart cards that would help simplify government business and bureaucracy. The smart cards would include an electronic healthcare card, a National ID card, and a Daily Living Card for services provided by local authorities. A significant part of ADELE is the migration of 10-15% of the Government's workstations to open source software in order to evaluate the possibilities this type of software might offer. The migration will include not only operating systems (Linux), but open source office (OpenOffice) and e-mail applications, databases (MySQL) and web browsers (Mozilla) as well. The reasons cited for the decision included cutting costs for licenses in order to spend more money on innovation, and increased security. The French Government plans to finish the migration process by 2007.

United Kingdom. The British Government has been very outspoken about its interest in the cost-cutting benefits of using open source software. In 2000, the Government carried out a study to analyze a migration to open source software. The results of the study were used to create guidelines for public administrations interested in open source software. The guidelines recommend that an objective comparison between open source and commercial solutions should be based on a value for money perspective. Furthermore, they indicated that the use of open standards could favour interoperability between products and solutions. Finally, they suggested the open source software model might be applied to the distribution of the results of public research and development. In 2000, the Office of Government Commerce, which was established in 2000 to help government agencies get the best value for their money from vendors, published a document in favour of the adoption of open source software. The reasons cited were not only reduced costs, but the interoperability guaranteed by open standards as a criteria to be used for future developments.

A major player in the British Government's open source policy has been the NHS (National Health Service). A fundamental part of the large-scale modernization plan started by the NHS in 2000 is the creation of "...a new technology infrastructure that will streamline operations, slash costs, significantly improve patient care, and allow medical practitioners and patients to communicate with each other securely and easily."[90] In December 2003, the agency announced it would launch a trial of a Linux-based system. The agency decided to make the switch in hopes of reducing costs and having increased flexibility and security in its information systems.

In October 2003, the Office of Government Commerce announced it would be carrying out nine IT trial projects using open source software in diverse government offices to compare costs and performance. The project came in response to the British Government's Open Source Policy, announced in Parliament in July 2003, which calls for government agencies to compare open source software and commercial software. The trial projects are coordinated by the Office of the e-Envoy and could be extended to other agencies as well. The project involves both open source servers (Linux) and some desktop applications and is being carried out in collaboration with IBM.

Spain. The Spanish Government has also been involved in promoting studies on open source software and migrations to open source software in the central and local governments. The first main project was called "The Virtual MAP". This aim of this project, started in 1999, was to connect all of the centres of the Ministry of Public Administration by installing Linux, Apache and other open source software products. The project was successful and led to increased and improved standardisation and a reduction in costs. Linux servers and some other open source products are now being used for the information systems at the Ministry of Home Affairs, The Senate and the Ministry of Justice although most workstations still use commercial desktop software.

In July 2001, the Senate decided it was important to ensure that all the Government's websites, documents and software be compatible with open source formats and products.

Another important initiative carried out by a public administration in Spain is the LinEx Project started by the regional government in the Extremadura region. GNU/LinEx, a Linux distribution with GNOME as a desktop (the official desktop of the GNU project), was developed to be used in all of the schools in the region and in public institutions as well. In addition, the region promotes the use of LinEx in businesses and at home. Part of the project included providing training for the 15,000 teachers who would have to make the switch. Extremedura is one of the poorer regions in Spain and the use of open source software was seen as a way to bring everyone into the Information Age regardless of where they live. Open source software was used because it offered the possibility to develop tailored software that could be reused and distributed at no cost.

Following the success of LinEx, the parliament in the independent region of Catalonia made a proposal to finance the development and production of open source software in the region as a way of stimulating the economy. In 2002, the Spanish Government announced another project, called Rodhas, that involved switching 8,000 more government workstations to Linux in order to save about 20 million Euro in software licenses.

Italy. In Italy, the Ministry for Innovation and Technologies have set up various initiatives to evaluate the possible benefits of using open source software. In 2000, the Italian Government approved a law that favoured the reuse of software in central and local governments. This law was seen as being in favour of open source software since open source licenses defend the principles of reusing and sharing software. In October 2002, the Ministry for Innovation and Technologies created a commission to study the technical, economic and organisational issues related to the use of open source software in Italian public administrations. At the end of the study, the commission published a report that discusses the applicability of open source software in the public sector and proposes some strategies for the procurement and use of software in the public sector. Among these proposals, the commission suggests that: open source software should be considered together with commercial software in a value for money assessment; public administrations must maintain full ownership of any software developed in or for their structures; reuse and sharing, interoperability based on standard interfaces, and vendor independence must be encouraged in public administrations; all documents issued by a public administration must be made available and recorded in at least one open format. These suggestions led the Ministry to set down the rules and criteria public administrations should use when buying and reusing software and officially recommend public administrations take open source software into consideration.

In January 2004, Tuscany became the first region in Italy to sign a law officially encouraging its local authorities to adopt open source software. Given the financial constraints public schools must deal with, the law gives particular attention to the adoption of open source software in public educational institutions in order to cut costs. Furthermore, the law states that any institution in the region that does migrate to open source will receive financial support from the region.

In February 2004, the City Council of Rome announced that it was going to carry out a gradual migration from commercial to open source software starting with the city's electronic mail system. Once again, the reasons cited were to cut costs and have greater flexibility.

Austria. Austria has set up many initiatives to develop e-government in the country, but for now the only one directly involving open source software is a proposal by the City of Vienna, made in September 2003, to consider migrating its 15,000 workstations to open source software. The project would involve gradually switching several hundred computers a year to evaluate the use of open source software.

Belgium. In Belgium, the Government has not developed an official policy towards open source software. Nonetheless, the Brussels region uses open source software to manage public data and information because of the greater security these products can offer. Furthermore, 30% of the workstations in the public administrations use open source software. Although this is still not the majority of workstations, these two examples indicate that the Government is open to considering the possibilities offered by open source software.

Sweden. Sweden, together with Denmark, hosts the largest Linux user's group in the world and has advanced e-government operations. However, until 2003 the use of open source software in government offices was quite limited. In 2003, the Government commissioned the Swedish Agency for Public Management to make suggestions regarding the use of open source software in the country's public administrations. The report highlighted the importance of using open standards both for the provision and internal development of software solutions in order to achieve maximum interoperability within a public administration, between the administration and the public and between different administrations. The report recommended open source software be considered not only for the offices of the local governments but for public schools as well.

Finland. In February 2004, The Finnish Ministry of Finance, Public Management Department, published a report recommending the use of open source software development methods for the development of applications tailored for the central and local governments. The report suggested that whether the administrations develop their own software or procure it, they should have access to the source code and the right to modify it. The main reasons cited for considering open source software were the possibility to tailor software and improve security.

Ireland. On April 29, 2004, the Minister in charge of the Information Society in Ireland announced the Irish Government's intention to launch an e-government program for the central infrastructure. Although the Government maintains the importance of using open standards, it clearly stated that this was not equivalent to using open source software. Furthermore, it claimed that using open source software might actually be too costly in the long-run. The announcement has opened a debate in the country on open source software. On May 4, Open Ireland, an open source software lobby group, sent an open letter to the Minister calling on the Government to develop an official policy towards open source software. Open Ireland claims that the benefits of using open source software in the public sector were transparency, reuse, open standards and lower costs.

Norway. In July, 2001, the state-owned company Statskonsult published a conclusive report following a study on Linux as an alternative to Windows in public administrations. The studied was carried out to consider ways to reduce vendor-dependency and the cost of buying software licenses. The report concluded that open source software has a lot of potential, but that at the time only Linux could be effectively implemented in public offices and schools given the lack of open source office applications then available.

In June 2004, the city council of Bergen, the second largest city in Norway, announced a decision to migrate its information system and school servers from Windows and Unix to Linux. The first part of the project will involve replacing 20 database servers that support the City's health and welfare applications with Linux. The second part will involve the City's educational network. The main reason for the decision was to free the city up from vendor dependence. Cost savings, possibility to customize the information infrastructure and more efficient operation were the other reasons cited for the move.

Russia. In October 2003, the Russian Ministry of Communications and Computerization announced that it would team up with IBM to create a Linux Competency Centre in Moscow. The aim of the Centre is to provide information on open source software to government agencies and business in Russia. In addition to the cost-savings factor, the Government expressed its belief that supporting the use of open source software in local businesses could help Russia hi-tech companies enter the global market.

Bulgaria. In June 2004, the United Nations Development Programme (UNDP) and the Internet Society of Bulgaria (ISOC-Bulgaria) launched a project to promote the use of open source software in the development of the country's e-government projects. The main aims are to improve government transparency and make it easier for citizens to access local government services and information. The Bulgarian government was already using open source software for large mail servers and database programs, but this project will focus on using open source software to complement the use of commercial desktop applications. The choice to use open source software was based on the belief that it will help local governments minimise the cost of buying and maintaining software. The project is expected to expand to other countries in South-Eastern Europe including Bosnia and Herzegovina, Croatia, Macedonia, Romania, Serbia and Montenegro.

7.4.2 Asian countries

In addition to the initiatives being carried out internally in different countries in Asia, there have been two major joint efforts by Japan,

China and South Korea to promote and develop open source software. At the end of 2003, the three Asian countries agreed to develop an operating system able to compete with Microsoft Windows. Government policy makers in the three countries indicated that their countries' dependence on Microsoft posed a serious risk from both the economic and security points of view. The project proposed developing an operating system based on Linux and other open source software so that it could be modified and diffused freely. The three countries also announced they would launch projects to work on developing open source desktop applications as well. The results of the collaboration will be implemented in critical areas of business and government service networks. In April 2004, they met in Beijing to discuss the methods to be used for the collaboration, the exchange of human resources, technology and standardization.

Following the agreement in 2003, two companies in Japan and China began to collaborate on Asianux, a Linux server operating system. The first beta version of Asianux 1.0, released in April 2004, was developed by China's Red Flag Software and Japan's Miracle Linux in collaboration with Oracle. By July 2004, news reports were indicating that South Korea was planning to become involved in Asianux as well. If it does, Red Flag, Miracle Linux and other open source supporters in Asia hope that Asianux could be considered the base Linux platform for the three governments' open source collaboration. More than 40 other hardware and application vendors, some major ones such as NEC, Hitachi and Hewlett-Packard, are participating in the project as well.

China. The Chinese Government maintains almost complete control of all sorts of media. For example, since 2001, to access an internet point, Chinese citizens must have an "internet identity card" which allows the Government to monitor their online activities. There are also filters and firewalls that monitor and block communications and censure sites, even some which do not actually have contents, such as Google.com. Furthermore, the Chinese Government is very cautious about using western software products, in particular Microsoft products, because of fears that there may be "back doors" westerners could use.

Interestingly, this wariness has actually helped promote policies to research and develop new, open source standards in China.

In its five-year plan (2001-2005), the technological innovation policy of the Chinese Government has two main aims: to free the Chinese market up from the dominant software and hardware companies and promote the development of its own standards. Although the Government authorized the release of Windows 2000 and Windows XP on the Chinese market, it does not use these products in its government offices. Beijing is already involved in several projects for developing its own software and standards. Since 2000, in collaboration with an association of Chinese software producers whose aim is to diffuse applications based on Linux and the help of Intel, the Ministry of Information has worked on building software assistance and development centres. AMD (a direct competitor to Intel) signed a joint venture with the China Basic Educational Software Company (CBE), a public company, to create CBE AMD Information Technology whose aim is to research and develop software applications for China's education market.

In December 2003, an agreement was made between the CSSC (China Standard Software Company), Sun Microsystems and the Ministry of Science and Technology to install up to 200 million copies of the Java Desktop System in both the public and private spheres. Under the agreement the CSSC will deliver its own branded products using the Java Desktop System, which is a Linux software bundle including GNOME, Mozilla and StarOffice. This agreement is seen as the foundation for a nation-wide standard based on open source software.

Japan. The first deadline of the Japanese Government's e-government strategy was April 2004 and neither this stage nor the future ones include a specific policy on open source software for e-government. Nonetheless, at the end of 2002, the Government created a commission of experts, including some Microsoft experts, to evaluate the advantages and disadvantages of migrating to open source software in the public sector. Following the agreement with China and South Korea in 2003, the Government announced it would spend 1 billion yen a year on the project and endorse an open source forum set up by Japan's major computer and electronics industry. At the end of April 2004, the Ministry of Economy, Trade and Industry (METI) announced a partnership with 19 companies, including NEC and IBM, to promote Linux use in the country's public schools. The aim of the project is to limit the dominance of Microsoft Windows in the public sector. As part of this pilot program, the companies involved will give a sample of secondary schools 500 Linux-equipped PCs. If the project is successful, METI intends to launch a project that would include companies as well in order to increase the diffusion of Linux in the country.

South Korea. At the end of 2003, the South Korean Ministry of Information and Communication announced a plan to migrate 20% of the Government's PCs and 30% of its servers to open source software by 2007. The project will involve thousands of computers in government ministries, universities and government-linked organisations. The Ministry expects the project will save the Government a significant amount of money, ensure security and improve interoperability.

Malaysia. In February 2004, the Malysian Government approved the Public Sector Open Source Software Masterplan which promotes the adoption of open source software in local governments. The Masterplan requires public administrations who need to procure software to carefully compare commercial and open source software on the basis of value for money, transparency, security and interoperability. It even goes as far to state that if the comparison proves the two products to be equal, the public administration should prefer the open source software solution. The Government estimates that by 2005, open source software, including everything from operating systems to desktop applications, will be installed on 60% of all new servers, 30% of office infrastructures and 20% of the computers used in school computer labs. Although many government agencies were already using open source software, a survey carried out in the first few months of 2004 indicated that open source software could be used more. In July, the Government launched the Open Source Competency Centre to serve as a point of reference for all open source software-related activities in the public sector, including everything from training to certification programs.

India. The Indian Government has not made any official policies regarding the adoption of open source software in government offices. As with other developing countries, the level of software consumption in India is extremely low and the level of piracy quite high. Nonetheless, India is unique in that it is the centre of software outsourcing for many multi-national companies. The fact that many Indians are employed by these companies to produce software means that India has the potential and human resources to develop its own software.

In 2002, the Department of Information Technology announced a strategy to introduce Linux and open source software as a standard in academic institutions in India. These institutions would be encouraged to carry out research on possible solutions and work on developing them so that they could be reused by the central and local governments. Furthermore, it indicated that government and academic institutions could collaborate with large software companies to carry out open source training and programming. The main reason cited for the promotion of open source software was to save money and make information technologies more accessible to more people through free reuse and distribution.

In 2003, the Department of Information Technology supported the development of Indix, a Hindi Linux distribution.

In 2004, the Indian State of Haryana announced that it had decided to migrate from Microsoft Windows to Sun Microsystems' StarOffice for all the state government departments. The decision was made in hopes of saving money on licensing and gaining vendor independence.

7.4.3 American countries

The only two American countries mentioned here are Brazil and the USA, but for very different reasons. Brazil has taken a strong stance on the issue of open source versus commercial software. It is strongly promoting the use of open source software throughout the country. Although the United States is the home of many of the movements and founders of free and open software, the Government has taken no position on the issue of open source software.

Brazil. Brazil is a developing country in which only 10% of the population of 170 million owns a computer. The Istituto Brasileiro de Geografia e Estatistica (IBGE) recently carried out a study which revealed that 92% the country's 180,000 public schools do not have internet access. What's worse is that half of the public schools don't even have a telephone line. The Lula Government came into office in 2002 with a public policy of defending "national interests" and a "new industrial policy". At the same time, the government sector had to cut costs extensively, to stay within the IMF spending limits and reach, and maintain, a primary surplus of 3.25% of its GNP. Developing and adopting open source software can help meet these goals. The Lula Government has stopped investing public money on new commercial software licenses.

In 2003, the Government announced a three-year pilot project to migrate many of the workstations in government offices to open source software, in particular Linux. The decision was based on lower costs, increased security, the promotion of local software production and facilitating access to knowledge. The Government has also planned to bring broadband internet access to its public schools, healthcare centres and public libraries using open source software. In the same year, the Government published guidelines for public administrations, universities and state companies that intend to migrate to open source software. The Brazilian Government has created the Digital Inclusion Program Brazil to help close the country's digital divide. The program has created community managed centres that offer free internet access using open source software. In April 2004, over 2000 civil servants met in Brasilia for training in using open source software, free of charge. The aim of the courses is not only to give the civil servants the skills they need to use open source software in government offices, but also to give them knowledge regarding open source software software that they can then share with the larger community.

In June 2004, the Brazilian state of Parana began a migration to open source software. The first part of the project involves a shift to a tailored version of eGroupWare, to be called Expresso, for e-mailing and other related functions for all 10,000 users in the Parana Government. Another part of the project, called Paranavegar, is aimed at using open source software to bring internet access and software courses to poorer communities in the state.

By August 2004, 20% of all computers used by the Brazilian ministries were running on Linux and other open source software. The Government plans to reach 100% by 2005.

In December 2003, IBM and the Brazilian Government announced an agreement to work on expanding the use of Linux in Brazil. In September 2004, the two signed another agreement to create a knowledge and technology centre for the development and promotion of open source software solutions. The centre will be involved in training and providing support to professionals and public administrations implementing open source software.

USA. The United States of America is home to many of the most important commercial software companies in the world. These companies are not inclined to accept open source software as a viable alternative to their products. They also have a significant influence in the political sphere in the United States. Needless to say, the number of initiatives involving open source software in the federal, state and local governments in the USA is much smaller than the number of initiatives in other major countries.

The Initiative for Software Choice (ISC) is a global coalition of companies and associations, based in the USA, whose aim is to promote "...neutral government procurement, standards and public R&D policies for software".[91] The ISC claims that when governments mandate a preference for open source software, they are actually harming competition and innovation in the software industry and market. The group is actively involved in fighting government decisions to adopt open source software, not only in the United States but in other countries around the world as well.

There is one state, however, that has been somewhat active in the debate on the use of open source software for governments and that state is Massachusetts. It may be no coincidence that Massachusetts is the only state, among the many that sued Microsoft, that has yet to accept an agreement. In September 2003, a memo by Eric Kriss, secretary of the Massachusetts Executive Office for Administration and Finance stated a series of drawbacks to using commercial software. Among these were the costs, vendor lock-in and dependence on outside consultants. The memo started a debate among state policy makers that ended in the creation of the "Enterprise Information Technology Acquisition Policy" for the state of Massachusetts. The document clearly differentiates between open standards and open source software. It states that all information technology solutions must be based on open standards but that commercial, public sector code sharing and open source solutions should all be evaluated. In March 2004, the state unveiled a software repository designed to let government agencies make more efficient use of open source software. The repository, which consists of various open source software solutions, will be housed at the University of Rhode Island and managed by the Government Open Code Collaborative. This group includes seven states and four municipalities that will contribute to developing and be able to download open-source and commercial solutions for the specific needs of government agencies. The reasons cited for the creation of the repository include avoiding vendor lock-in, saving tax-payers money and increasing interoperability between different government agencies.

Several other states, including Oregon and California, have made proposals for the adoption of open source software. However, for now all of these proposals have died, often with the justification that the state government should not mandate open source software as the only choice for state agencies and public administrations.

What this overview has hopefully made clear is that in just five years, the interest governments around the world have started to show in open source software has increased significantly. While some governments are still developing their policies towards open source software, others have begun installing it on a large scale. It is also worth noting that in some cases, local governments have been setting up their own open source software initiatives, we could say, from the bottom up. The first initiatives served as a sort of example as to what could potentially be done, making it easier for other local governments to follow suit. All of these initiatives are subject to rapid changes that are a result of the dynamic nature of the ICT industry itself, the legal issues regarding open source software, such as the software patent controversy, and the social-political culture in each country.

So far in this book, we have made a relatively practical analysis of the open source software phenomenon and its impact on the ICT industry and government policies. The aim of the next two chapters is to take a look at the phenomenon from a more theoretical point of view. We will see how the open source software phenomenon can be used as an example of more widespread changes that are taking place in organizations and society today.

Chapter 8

New Trends in Work Organization

8.1 Work Organization: The Open Source Community versus Commercial Companies

As we have already seen in Chapter 1, a well-known comparison made by Eric Raymond uses the metaphor of the cathedral and the bazaar to describe the organizational model for software development used in the commercial world and the one used in the open source community. The concepts of hierarchy, order, control, planning and a closed system with well-defined boundaries are associated with the cathedral and, consequently, commercial companies. The concepts of disorder, autonomy, free access, openness and self-organization are the characteristics that describe the bazaar and the open source community.

From this basic distinction, we can go one step further and identify a fundamental difference between companies and the open source community: the former are *organization centric* and the latter *project centric*. In a commercial company, the organization, or company, is at the centre and both projects and the formal work organization derive from the overall organizational setting. In this context, projects can only be set up if there is an established organizational setting. We could therefore say that there are no projects if there is no organization. On the other hand, in the open source community, the project and the informal networks of relationships that grow up around them are prerequisites for the existence of the community. The community develops as a result of the projects and without the projects there is merely a potential community. Projects are also what help the resources of the community from becoming dispersed and unable to focus on precise objectives. Projects are so important that they become the name for the part of the community involved in it. For example, we speak of the Linux community when referring to those working on the Linux project. Therefore, in the case of the open source community, we could say that there is no community if there are no projects (Figure 8.1).

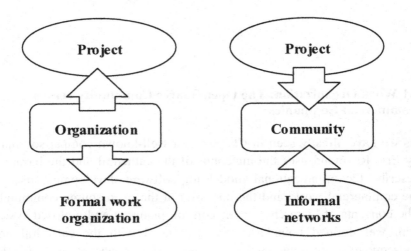

Figure 8.1 – Organization centric versus project centric approaches.

A quick glance at Figure 8.1 might give the impression that commercial businesses and the open source community are the antithesis of one another. In order to determine whether or not this is actually the case, we will consider six organizational aspects: the focus, information flow, resource selection, decision-making power, leadership and value system (see Table 8.1).

Commercial businesses tend to focus on their internal organization and its efficiency. Development activities are organized according to precise rules that aim to make managing activities simple and efficient. Organization is optimized in order to manage all projects with the same efficiency and effort. This is why we say these businesses are organization centric. On the contrary, the focus in the open source community is on the project; the single project is optimized rather than the organization. The organization of the community changes continuously depending on the projects and specific development needs of each project. This is why the organization of the open source community can be defined *project centric*.

Table 8.1 – Comparison between commercial companies and the open source community.

	Commercial Companies	The open source community
Focus	Organization-centric Development processes are not optimized for single projects.	Project-centric The development process is optimized for each single project.
Information Flow	Formal work organization Structured channels of communication. Limited flexibility.	Informal networks Flexible channels of communication within a network of relationships.
Resource Selection	Selection and hiring Personnel are hired and assigned to projects according to precise rules. Personnel must be carefully selected and trained.	Self-selection Software developers voluntarily choose to contribute to a project. There is no need for a formal process of selection and training.
Decision-making power	Top-down approach Potentially slow decision-making process can limit the innovative content of products.	Bottom-up approach Many different alternatives can be explored, speeding up development and leading to innovation.
Leadership	Experience and seniority Decision-making power in the hands of few.	Meritocracy Leadership based on trust and consensus.
Value System	Focus on profits Potential contrast between profits and product quality.	Freedom and merit Greater potential to have high quality products.

Information and knowledge flows are usually carefully defined in companies whereas in the open source community there are no predetermined paths. In companies, the structured channels of communication can create inertia in responding to technological and market changes. The organization of the open source community is freed up from these constraints. The main channels of communication for the informal networks of relationships are the various tools available on the Internet such as forums, chat rooms and mailing lists. This way of exchanging information and knowledge leads to the dynamism and flexibility that make the open source development process suitable for products and markets in continuous evolution.

The level and quality of competences in an organization are of fundamental importance in companies and, therefore, the main aims of the resource selection process are to search for the best possible competences and keep them. Personnel are allocated within the organization in such a way as to optimize how competences are used. In the open source community personnel selection is not based on any formal evaluation process. Programmers join the community because they are interested in a project, and they can leave a project whenever they want to. Competences are allocated using a merit-based self-selection mechanism which assigns roles and responsibilities in an implicit way.

In companies, decision-making takes place almost exclusively at the upper levels of a hierarchical structure (top-down approach). In the open source community, responsibilities are decentralized (bottom-up approach). In the top-down approach, the decision-making process tends to be slower, and this can limit the innovation process. On the contrary, in the bottom-up approach, programmers have greater autonomy to propose and develop original ideas, increasing the level of innovation of products and speeding up development. Anyone can contribute to the development process by studying and improving existing code and proposing new code.

In the companies, leadership is usually based on experience and seniority and the decision-making power is in the hands of a few people. Leadership is relatively stable over time, but static as well. In the open source community people come to be considered leaders only if they have the right mix of merit, trust and consensus. This mechanism makes leadership the subject of continuous attention and revision. Consequently, the leadership is temporary and relatively unstable. However, this mechanism reduces potentially opportunistic behaviours since the community would pick up on them and not tolerate them.

The value system in companies is influenced by the pursuit of economic profit, which could, in some cases, prove to be in contrast with the pursuit of high quality processes and products. The open source community, on the other hand, is made up of programmers who voluntarily contribute to developing products. As has already been seen in Chapter 3, two of the main motivating factors for programmers in the community are the challenge of solving a problem and the acquisition of reputation capital. Programmers are motivated to develop high quality products because they have the freedom to work on what interests them and the only thing they have to gain is improved reputation capital.

8.2 Changes in Organizational Models

For much of the twentieth century, organizational models were based on the Fordist model. Significant changes really only began to take place during the last two decades of the century. The main drivers of these changes were the diffusion of information and communication technologies. As a result, organizations have changed the way they operate. Four characteristics in particular help describe these changes: network structure, temporary organization of activities, virtual setting, and trust-based relationships (Table 8.2).

Table 8.2 – Comparison of organizational models.

	Traditional (Fordist) Model	Project Based Networks	Open Source Community
Resources	Ownership of resources	Access to resources	Independence from resources
Location	Place	Cluster	Space
Management of Projects	Company Based Projects	Project Based Organization	Project Centric Community
Governance	Control of resources	Trust and rules posed by formal contracts	Informal rules and trust
Identity	Organizational culture and values	Portfolio of relationships	Values and culture of the professional community

The concept of working in networks is certainly not new, but new information and communication technologies have allowed many different types of organizations to adopt network structures. A network structure obviously functions differently from more traditional hierarchical structures but two aspects in particular characterize new organizations today: accessing, not owning, resources and working by projects.

In a network structure access to resources is more important than owning them. The concept of having access to resources indicates a tendency to avoid, as much as possible, owning resources in order to use resources only when they are necessary and only for the shortest time required. These resources make up the so-called *just in time capital,* i.e. a form of capital that can be used on a needs-only basis. This not only means that outsourcing all types of resources is becoming more and more common, but that the very concept of outsourcing has actually been modified. In fact, in a network logic, outsourcing becomes co-sourcing in the sense that both the supplier and host organization participate in the production of resources. Both are at the same time suppliers and customers of resources.[92]

The logic of having access to resources rather than owning them goes hand in hand with the logic of working by projects. A project is a temporary effort made to create a unique product or service. We can say "temporary" because a project has a specific beginning and end. We can say "unique" because the aim of a project is to develop products or services that have new features that do not exist in other products or services. Therefore, a project can be defined as a set of activities characterized by defined objectives, limited resources and time constraints. The defined time frame of each project becomes the time limit of the network itself. Once a project is finished, the network ceases to exist and new projects create a new network. The network changes shape continuously since the individual members can come together with others to create new networks and develop new projects.

The importance of working by projects has increased as a result of the increase in the complexity of technologies and products, the need to integrate different functions, the shortening of time-to-market and the dynamics of the market demand. Consequently, flexibility, i.e. the ability to organize activities on a short-term basis and quickly move resources from one objective to another, has also become more important.[93]

From a management style that focuses on the characteristics of single projects there has been a move to the concept of project management as an organizational philosophy. In other words, the logic behind project management is used not only to manage projects but many other organizational activities as well. The diffusion of a project-centred organizational approach and the intrinsic temporary nature of projects mean that the activities of organizations, and in some cases even their structure, are becoming more and more temporary.

Another characteristic of organizations today is that they are making more use of virtual settings. The concept of a virtual organization emerged with the development of information technologies as they broadened the organizational "space". In a virtual organization there is no precise physical location where or time when activities are carried out. In fact, a virtual organization works in a *space* rather than in a *place*. Activities do not take place at the same time in the same place. The fact that activities no longer depend on space and time means that virtual organizations can work anywhere and without time constraints. In this context, "[w]ork is what you do, not where you go".[94] The new workspace is an information space without place and time constraints. Activities are carried out using digital technologies and electronic or virtual workspaces are created.[95] In fact, in a virtual setting, resources are information contents in a digital format (bits), not physical objects (atoms). Virtual organizations concentrate above all on intellectual work and, therefore, human capital is the organization's main asset.

Network structures, the temporary organization of activities and virtual settings give organizations greater flexibility and consequently some advantages. Nonetheless, organizations founded on these characteristics tend to be much less structured than more traditional ones. These organizations take on the characteristics of a community. To work well they need two integration mechanisms: governance and identity. Both of these mechanisms are based on trust.

The word governance refers to the set of mechanisms used to govern and control resources and activities. Whereas governance based on command and control prevails in traditional organizations, in virtual and temporary organizations a governance based on trust prevails ("trust to make it work"). Nonetheless, trust does not come about automatically, but must be created, understood, managed and recognized by everyone in the organization.[96] In organizations today, people's knowledge, skills and inter-personal relationships are becoming more and more important. People's ability to relate to one another depends on sharing common social norms and values and the ability to put one's own personal interest aside for the interest of the group as a whole. Trust is created when a group shares some values. Trust increases people's desire to work within a group to achieve common goals. It is the expectation created within a community that people will behave in a predictable, appropriate and cooperative way according to norms shared by all the community's members. If this expectation does not exist, people must be obliged to respect formal and explicit rules.[97] Trust, therefore, plays an important role in achieving goals in the context of virtual and temporary organizations.

Trust also plays a role in helping create and maintain a group's sense of identity. Organizations based on trust are different from more traditional ones in that they have a new concept of identity. In traditional organizations, identity is based on an existing organizational culture and members of the organization must adapt to these pre-established values. On the contrary, the new identity in virtual and temporary organizations is a set of dynamic values that grows out of the interaction between individuals. In this case, identity is based on a dynamic, diversified and fragmentary system of values that is continuously being built and modified.[98]

All of the changes we have discussed so far characterize the organization of the open source community. In fact, the open source community can be considered a new archetype for organizations that is based on a different definition of the boundaries between an organization and its environment. In order to understand how it is different, we will compare the open source community with the Fordist model and the project based network model. The comparison considers five key aspects: resources, location, how projects are managed, governance and identity.

As far as resources are concerned, organizations that use the traditional model try to own resources and keep them for long periods of time. On the contrary, the open source community is against owning resources because it is not owning but rather the freedom to share resources that gives the community value. Project based networks are between these two extremes. The added value of this type of network comes from the possibility to access resources, i.e. the ability to bring together the most suitable resources at the right time and for the right amount of time (just in time capital).

As far as location is concerned, traditional organizations tend to concentrate resources in one or few places in order to control processes and limit communication costs and time. In the open source community, on the other hand, the place of work is simply any number of places where in any given moment programmers are working on open source projects. In other words, it is not people who are moving to the place of work, but information that is being transferred via the internet. Since all of the members of the community are independent, resources cannot be carefully controlled. Therefore, the community does not have a place of work but rather a workspace, the internet. In project based networks the need to control the network is limited by the fact that the project is itself a form of control in that it guides the efforts towards achieving precise goals. What ties together the various players that make up the network is the fact that they are pursuing common objectives. In this case, the location can be represented using the concept of cluster.

In order to compare how projects are managed, we can identify three different approaches: company based project, project based organization and project centric community. In the traditional model, projects are company based in that they depend on the overall organization of the company. The open source community, on the other hand, is a project centric community. This means that the make-up of the community and how it is organized depends entirely on the projects. The communities are built up around projects and not only are the projects temporary, but so is the make-up of the group of people working on a given project as they can enter and exit the community whenever they want to. Between these two extremes is a project based way of organizing activities, which is characteristic of project based networks. Similar to a more traditional company there is a core organizational cluster, but like the open source community, the way the activities and resources are organized varies from one project to another.

The concept of governance that prevails in the traditional model is command and control, i.e. the formal control of resources and activities in order avoid unsuitable and opportunistic behaviors and ensure that the activities are carried out in the correct manner. On the contrary, in the open source community, proper functioning is guaranteed by informal rules and, above all, the trust that each player places in and expects of the others. A project based network uses each of these governance mechanisms to some degree. Although trust is indispensable for building a network, in a project based network some rules must be formalized in order to ensure the activities are carried out in the correct manner. These rules are defined by formal contracts that last, however, only as long as the project does.

In the traditional model, identity is created by establishing a stable and coherent system of values that makes up what we call organizational culture. In the open source community, on the other hand, the members of the community do not identify themselves with a company. The sense of identity comes from belonging to a community of professionals and hobbyists who share similar experiences and values. In a project based network, identity comes from the relationships between professionals within and outside of the network itself, creating a portfolio of relationships. Professionals identify with the network and, therefore, the identity varies according to the structure and composition of the network. The sense of identity is temporary, or better, very dynamic and diversified because it depends on networks that are continuously being built and modified.

Even though it may be too soon to say that the open source community is a new organizational model, the organizational mechanisms that characterize it may have an influence on more consolidated organizational models. The factors that seem particularly significant are the way in which projects are carried out, the dynamic comings and goings of members of the community depending on the interest projects attract, and the importance of the integration mechanisms based on trust. Finally, as we will see later in this chapter, the influence of these factors may move beyond organizations and communities and have an impact on the broader social context as well.

8.3 Changes in the Way People Work

The way work is organized in the open source community is merely an extreme example of more general changes taking place in work organization today. In the case of the open source community, the expression 'work organization' might seem paradoxical. The development activities carried out by the members of the community cannot be considered a job in the traditional sense of the word since the work is carried out by volunteers. Nonetheless, open source programmers do work to create actual products, even if not necessarily as a part of their job.

In Chapter 3, we saw that the factors that motivate open source programmers to contribute to open source projects for free and on a voluntary basis can be ethical, political, social and only indirectly economic (e.g. reputation capital). Some of the most common motivating factors given by programmers are the desire to satisfy specific needs, the pure fun of programming and the acquisition of reputation capital. The pleasure that comes from programming is similar to the pleasure one gets from carrying out scientific research or doing artistic activities. In fact, we can use the word 'work' for research and artistic activities as well. Words that come to mind to describe this type of work are pleasure, absorption and dedication. 'Work' in the more widely accepted sense of the word tends, on the contrary, to be associated with attributes such as uninteresting, boring or oppressive.

In the following paragraphs, we will see how there is a growing trend to organize work so that it is more similar to 'work' in the sense of pleasure. This trend is related to a transformation in the way people work that has taken place as a result of the transition from an industrial economy where manual work prevailed, to a knowledge economy where intellectual work prevails. First of all, there is a growing trend of work being freed up from time and place constraints. In the case of intellectual work, a specific place of work and synchronized activities are no longer needed. Secondly, in today's knowledge economy, work is becoming more and more autonomous and individuals are focusing more on their visibility on the professional market (marketability). Knowledge workers prefer to have a more autonomous, flexible, subjective, decentralized and, above all, creative job. Furthermore, their motivation depends on how much passion they have for the work they do. We can even go as far as to say that there is a new work ethic which places more importance on enjoying what you do rather than working for the sole purposes of having a job and earning money.

8.3.1 Time and place

Traditionally, work is constrained by time and place. There is a time for work and a place for work. When we talk about work time we are distinguishing this from free time. In other words, time is organized in such a way as to separate work activities from activities that help restore the physical and mental conditions needed to work again.

Traditionally we organize our work and rest time according to the well-known Benedictine rule which calls for canonical activities for each hour of the day.[99] The temporal distinction between work and idleness comes from the ethic stated by the Benedictine rule: "idleness is the enemy of the soul".

The formal organization and optimization of work time tend to be quite strict. Activities are carried out within predefined time intervals and must be sequenced and synchronized with other activities. The sequencing and synchronization of work times influence not only people's work lives but their social lives outside of work as well. In fact, people are forced to divide up their personal time in a precise and formal way.

The alternative to this way of organizing time is to "de-sequence" activities, which consequently makes synchronization less important.[100] This is what happens in the open source community where there is no formal organization of work. The programmers autonomously decide when to work and, therefore, how to organize their time. In this context, sequencing and synchronization are no longer relevant because the optimization of the activities does not regard time but rather only results.

The absence of a precise organization of work times can lead to a lack of a clear distinction between work time and free time. This might disprove the Benedictine rule by which "idleness is the enemy of the soul" and support, vice versa, the concept of "creative idleness" or "productive idleness".[101]

Not only is the concept of work time changing, but organizations are changing the concept of work space and place as well. The quantity and quality of the intellectual work done nowadays are less tied down to specific places of production. Furthermore, a focus on results rather than work reduces the need to control work times. The reduced importance of work place makes it possible to increase the distances between the actual place where work is being done and where organizational decisions are being made. With new information technologies the physical distances between these two places is no longer an issue thus broadening the work space.

If the results of work are knowledge products, then organizations can make more and more use of an "information space" rather than a physical space. This change leads to a significant structural transformation since the organizational space becomes a global space where what moves is information, not people. In this way workers do not have to actually go to a particular place to work, but rather there is a movement of information towards the workers wherever they are.

What are the drawbacks to this type of delocalization? Possible effects on individual workers are the need to carefully and effectively manage their time and excessive isolation from what goes on in the company. The drawback for organizations could be significant difficulties controlling the work process, the need to revolutionize its own value system, and a loss of company identity. There could be negative effects on society as well, such as the danger of social atomization and widespread work insecurity. However, the advantages of not having one specific place of work are not only the obvious ones of reducing or even eliminating the constraints of a workplace, as well as the positive effects that come from reducing other constraints, above all constraints on time and autonomy. Although the advantages of delocalization have yet to be accurately verified empirically, we do know that, for example, some advantages can be: increased productivity, changes in the social relationships within organizations, a better ratio of work time to free time, and the fact that workers take more responsibility for their own professional development.

8.3.2 Work autonomy

The new knowledge economy has produced significant changes in the structure of the contractual relationships between companies and knowledge workers. In particular, there is an ever-increasing use of flexible resources and, therefore, non-traditional forms of employment such as part-time, temporary work, etc.[102]

The traditional employment model is based on controlling resources, competences and knowledge. This model can be integrated, and in part substituted, by a logic of transaction that focuses on flexibility, i.e. look for what is needed when it is needed. In this context, work is evaluated based on the results it provides and not on how well resources have been used to produce results.

In order to understand this new logic of transaction, we need to look at the different types of contracts between companies and knowledge workers. What differentiates contracts is the level of the knowledge contents and how company-specific the contents are. Table 8.3 shows a classification of four types of contracts according to the level and specificity of the knowledge involved.

Table 8.3 – Types of contractual relationships (Adaptation from: Burton-Jones, 1999).

Knowledge specificity Level of the knowledge	Low	High (firm specific)
Low	Mediated Service Workers	Flexihires
High	Independent Contractors and Free Agents	Employees

When activities deal with a low level of knowledge, two types of employment contracts, both of which are flexible, can be used. Mediated services can be used when the knowledge is not particularly firm-specific. These workers do not have contracts directly with the firm, but rather through a services company, e.g. security. However, when the knowledge is very firm-specific, the firm must have greater control over the results of the work while at the same time maintaining a certain degree of flexibility. In this case firms use flexible hires and other types of employment contracts such as part-time, temporary work, etc.

In the case of a high level of knowledge, firms turn to independent contractors when the knowledge is not firm-specific and hire employees when it is. The contracts stipulated between independent contractors and firms are explicit and result-oriented. These contracts are transaction oriented. The knowledge that is dealt with is less critical for a firm's competitiveness but nonetheless very important. This knowledge may deal with legal and financial issues, information technology and even planning and design. These contracts lead to diffused phenomena of self-employment. Consultants and free agents make up this group.[103] The term free agent refers both to the contents of the work done (they are knowledge workers) and the type of contract stipulated. Free agents are usually highly skilled professionals who prefer to work independently on various projects for several different organizations. Employees, on the other hand, have a more traditional contract with the company because they have a high level of knowledge which is very firm-specific. In this way, the company has greater control but less flexibility.

These new forms of contracts may lead to situations that could be potentially negative. For example, the use of temporary work contracts could lead workers to feel a sense of anxiety and precariousness and less economic security. Furthermore, companies could take advantage of these types of contracts to the harm of workers. This over-use of temporary workers has grown especially in firms that employ contingent high-tech workers. An example of this is the so-called "permatemps" phenomenon, i.e. workers that are permanently temporary. Though these workers have a certain continuity in their employment for the same firm, they are tied to the firm by temporary contracts and cannot therefore benefit from all of the rights guaranteed to full-time employees.

These new forms of employment produce an overall increase in worker autonomy. The main consequences of this increase in autonomy are a reduced sense of belonging and loyalty to an organization, the need to work in different organizations during one's life, a reduction in the specificity and importance of the contents of the work done, and the increased importance of life-long learning. The loss of loyalty[104] means that individual workers tend to move from firm-reliance to self-reliance. This lack of belonging to an organization is made up for by a new sense of belonging and loyalty to a group of professionals. This shift also creates a need to develop skills that are not particularly specific to any single project or firm. These new workers need to continuously become involved in new projects. Consequently, they must develop general skills and knowledge that can be exploited in as broad a context as possible, skills that can then be fine-tuned for each new project. Furthermore, in order to work for many different organizations, these workers have to develop a tight network of contacts and negotiate their own skills with firms.[105]

This trend leads towards the development of a phenomenon that can be called "dejobbing". In dejobbing, work is centred around the specific needs of single projects rather than predefined job contents. In this context, workers must have a set of competences that can be exploited for different projects and tasks.

Finally, greater autonomy and changes in job structure produce a different way of conceiving professional development. In traditional jobs, it is the organization that manages each individual worker's professional development. In the new context of work autonomy and self-employment workers themselves must be responsible for their own continuous learning and marketability.

8.3.3 Creativity, passion and quality of work

The quality of work is related to the intrinsic creative content of the work itself and the passion that the work inspires in those who do it.[106]

Creativity is the ability to invent or produce original, imaginative or inventive work or ideas. Creative people use their intuition and creativity to bring together different ideas and knowledge in order to propose new solutions. In a work context, two elements influence people's creativity: experience and motivation. Experience can be defined as a person's cultural, intellectual and professional background or a person's "intellectual space". There are two basic types of motivations: external motivations, e.g. economic incentives, and internal motivations, which are a positive attitude towards the activities one carries out. Economic incentives do not necessarily induce creative behaviour in people. On the other hand, creativity is favoured when people feel passionate about, are interested in, and are satisfied and challenged by what they are doing. People are more creative when they are moved by internal motivations, i.e. motivated by their own personality and by the positive perception they have of what they do.

The quality of work is also influenced by whether or not the work makes people feel passionate about what they do. The perception of quality is negatively influenced when people feel that their work is a burden and when a job generates dissatisfaction. If, however, we feel passionate about what we do, then we achieve what Mihaly Csikszentmihalyi calls flow experience. Flow experience is a situation in which the attention and concentration needed to reach a given objective come about automatically. In some ways the involvement in the activity actually decreases the amount of stress and helps increase concentration. Work can become a flow experience and therefore a "source of joy" or flow activity. When this happens work becomes a source of satisfying experiences and one's involvement becomes total. Basically, making work a flow activity is the best way to exploit people's creative potential.[107]

Work can also become a joyful experience if people feel that it offers them opportunities for personal improvement, i.e. if in addition to economic gratification there is also, and above all, satisfaction in doing the work. In order for this to happen, work must take on the characteristics of a flow activity. People have to learn to recognize the right opportunities, refine their skills and look for suitable goals.

In some cases, creativity is actually considered to be in conflict with the fundamental principles of business. Creativity is often neglected in order to focus on productivity and controlling work activities. Nonetheless, it is possible to relate these business principles to creativity and attain the so-called business creativity. Business creativity is not related only to the degree to which ideas are original, but to the utility and applicability of the ideas as well.

What then are the obstacles to effectively exploiting creativity? Teresa Amabile has identified two main obstacles, one related to organizational culture and the other to the pressure to speed up work times.[108] Sometimes organizational culture can obstruct the development and exploitation of creativity. This happens when organizations do not seem to be interested in new ideas or changes or when they stimulate internal competition too much. Creativity cannot be developed under these conditions because it would be considered too risky. The pressure to get things done in a limited amount of time can also obstruct creativity as it might push people to reach a goal regardless of whether or not creative solutions have been sought or considered. Too much pressure to reduce project times has a negative influence on creative activities such as learning, exploration, brainstorming, and coming up with and testing new concepts, ideas and procedures.

Is there a difference between work time and creative time? Obviously work time does not always coincide with creative time. Intuitions and creative ideas can come to one's mind at any time and, therefore, outside predefined work time. Therefore, work time must become more flexible in order to allow creativity to emerge.

Creativity, understood as the ability to come up with new ideas and to make them happen while at the same time making a profit off of them, is required in all those activities that involve innovation and entrepreneurship. Creativity is the distinguishing characteristic of certain types of activities and industries. The categories of people whose work is almost entirely dedicated to very creative activities have been called the creative class. Richard Florida defines the creative class as a group of creative people working in various industries, most often industries dealing with a significant amount of knowledge content.[109] The creative class has to deal with complex problems and finding the solutions requires significant effort, competences, judgement and personal initiative. In other words, creativity is particularly important when ability and talent are required to carry out activities.

8.3.4 Work ethic

The way work is carried out in the open source community has also shed more light on a new philosophy or ethic of work. The new work ethic is that of the community, or as Pekka Himanen's has called it, the hacker ethic.[110] The hacker ethic opposes the protestant work ethic theorized by Max Weber in his work *The Protestant Ethic and the Spirit of Capitalism*. According to Weber, the protestant ethic derives from the organization of life inside a monastery. In a monastery, work is not important because it gives results but it is good because it keeps people from away from idleness, which is the enemy of the soul. According to this view, not only is work a duty but there is also an economic reward for working. Therefore, the protestant ethic is very much related to money. The hacker ethic, on the other hand, is an ethic based on pleasure and money is not the most important thing. The work programmers do for open source projects is a "non-job" that they do for pleasure and entertainment. Linus Torvalds himself started the Linux project saying it was "just a hobby". Raymond as well highlights the playful aspect and passion that characterize this type of work: "You need to care. You need to play. You need to be willing to explore."[111] Some of the values this new ethic is based on are passion, freedom, openness, and the social value of one's activities.

The precursor to this new ethic is not the monastery but rather academia. In academia people are motivated by a passion for the search of new knowledge as well as the desire to improve their reputation within the scientific community. The results of scientific research do not only have value for the person who did the work but a social value as well. Since the number of people dedicated to scientific activities is very limited, one could object that a work ethic based on these principles is utopian and would have little impact on the way work is conceived in other contexts. However, though traditional types of labour may not have much in common with the way the scientific community works, knowledge-based activities and jobs do. If we use the knowledge contents of various activities as a reference, we can imagine that the influence of this new work ethic could very well move beyond the limits of scientific activities.

In today's knowledge society, work has become more and more an intellectual rather than physical activity. In intellectual activities, intelligence and creativity cannot easily be substituted by technological instruments. Therefore, we cannot say that work is destined to disappear as it is substituted by technology, but rather that the concept and principles of work must change. Rather than an "end of work" as predicted by Jeremy Rifkin, we can speak of the "end of a concept of work", a concept based on the idea that work can be substituted by technology. Work is becoming something else and it is taking on characteristics that could be defined "non work" at least until a new concept is not established as part of a common way of thinking or a culture.[112]

These considerations on work ethic relate to, and in some ways sum up, all of the previous considerations made regarding time, space, creativity, passion, etc. The model of work is changing and it is being influenced by new ways of organizing time, space, creative contents, but most of all by the consideration, or desire, that work be a passion and not only a duty.

8.4 Towards New Organizational Models

The trends and changes that we have discussed in this chapter seem to indicate that there may be new organizational models. At the one extreme we have the traditional Fordist industrial model and at the other extreme we have the characteristics that are typical of open source software development activities. Current changes that are taking place in the way work is organized fall between these two extremes. We will now compare these three categories by considering the aspects discussed in this chapter: work time and place/space, autonomy, worker identity, motivations and work ethic (Table 8.4).

The traditional model is based on a formal organization of time. In other words, work time is precisely defined in order to maximize production. In this case there is a distinct separation between work time and free time. This type of organization of time is applied to all of those activities that cannot be "de-sequenced". The more activities become

Table 8.4 – Characteristics of different types of work organization.

	Traditional (Fordist) Model	**Current changes in work organization**	**Open source community**
Time	Formal organization of time. Separation between work time and free time.	Flexible organization of time. More control over division of work time and free time.	Individuals organize their own time. Overlap between "work time" and free time.
Place/ Space	Precise, physical place of work determines the mobility of physical resources and workers.	Delocalized workplace (move physical resources) and/or virtual workplace (move information)	Virtual workspace driven by the digital exchange of information.
Autonomy	Hierarchical organization	Self-employment	Self-involvement
Identity	Company	Professional associations	Community of professionals
Motivations	Tangibile: Pay and work stability	Independence and flexibility	Intangible: personal satisfaction and improved reputation
Ethic	Protestant Ethic Work as a duty	Freelancer Ethic Work as a series of opportunities	Hacker Ethic Work as a passion

intellectual activities, the less the formal rules of the traditional model hold true. In the open source community there are no formal work times. The independence of the programmers and the absence of a formal organization allow programmers to organize their own activities and work time. In this case there is often an overlap between work time and free time, i.e. many programmers "work" on open source projects during their free time. The way work time is organized (or not organized) in the open source community cannot easily be applied to business activities. Nonetheless, in some industries working in knowledge products, work time could be organized in a more flexible way giving workers more control over when to work and when to have free time.

In the traditional model there is a defined, physical work place that physical resources and workers must be brought to. On the contrary, in the open source community there is a work *space* that is not clearly defined because it is virtual. The main resources are information and the virtual workspace is an information space. Since information is exchanged via the Internet, the information is almost impossible to control. Therefore, the workspace cannot be identified in any specific place. New ways of organizing work tend to exploit both place and space. To move physical resources, the workplace can be delocalized and to move information, virtual workspaces created.

The traditional employer-employee relationship has also undergone a transformation. In the traditional model, employees have a formal relationship with the organization. The position and responsibilities of each employee are clearly defined and determined by hierarchies. On the contrary, in the open source community, the concepts of hierarchy and being employed no longer exist since programmers voluntarily opt to participate in the projects that interest them (*self-involvement*). In the workplace today, where the number of temporary workers and free agents is steadily increasing, the concept of self-employment is becoming more and more commonplace.

Increased autonomy in the workplace has influenced workers' sense of identity and belonging to a group. In the traditional model, the sense of belonging is tied to a company, and work time and place. The exact opposite takes place in the open source community where the autonomy of the programmers makes it difficult to have a sense of belonging to an organization. In fact, programmers identify with the development community, i.e. a group of people who share the same experiences, competences and motivations. In new forms of organization, greater autonomy means that new ways of creating a sense of identity and belonging must be found. For example, professional organizations and associations can be a stable point of reference for members, guaranteeing support and services. This helps create social interaction and a sense of professional identity.

Another aspect that differentiates these three forms of organization is what motivates people to prefer one form over another. The main motivating factors for working for a traditional organization are generally tangible, i.e. pay and stability. On the contrary, the main motivating factors for open source programmers are intangible and based on personal values. As we have already seen, what motivates a development community to work for free is related to passion (*joy of hacking*), personal satisfaction and a sort of investment in one's future (*reputation capital*). Though these motivations may lead to economic gains in the future, they certainly do not lead to economic stability in the present. Once again there are changes taking place today that lie somewhere in between these two extremes. The independence and flexibility of new types of employment are not completely in contrast with the economic motivations of the traditional model and at the same time they may leave more room for more passion, satisfaction and creativity.

The ethics that underly these different forms of organization are quite different. In the traditional model, the ethic is based on the protestant ethic which defines work as a duty. In the open source community we speak of the hacker ethic, according to which work should be a passion, not an obligation. Between these two very different ways of interpreting work we have an ethic we could define as the freelancer ethic. Work keeps its professional importance, but passion and interest are important as well. The most important values are flexibility, meant as the possibility to change, and the sense of belonging to a network of professional and social relationships.

The traditional model is basically a very rigid model. Well-defined work time and place and limited autonomy leave people little freedom. On the other hand, it does guarantee people sufficient stability and tends to minimize the risk factors for the organization.

Work in the open source community is carried out in a very elastic, flexible way. People have greater freedom and fewer limitations on their creativity. Although the success of many open source products proves that these characteristics are positive and worth promoting, participation in the open source community is on a voluntary basis and can thus offer none of the guarantees traditional employment does.

Current changes in work organization seem to be looking for a compromise between the freedom offered by the open source community and the stability guaranteed by the traditional model. There is a focus on concepts related to freedom such as flexibility, delocalization and temporariness. At the same time, belonging to associations and networks helps guarantee these new knowledge workers some stability and security.

8.5 Impact on Social Capital

So far in this chapter we have taken a look at the organizational characteristics of the open source community as well as changes that are taking place in other knowledge-based sectors. In particular, we have seen that there is a trend towards more virtual and temporary ways of organizing work. But is there a downside to this new type of organization? What effects might organizations that are more and more virtual and temporary have on a social level? Can virtual and temporary organizations, which produce a "breaking up" effect and create the fragmentation of place, space and time, be considered to work against building and maintaining the so-called social capital?

In order to understand what social capital is, we must first take a look at how social groups are formed. The creation of social groups is the result of an implicit contract stipulated between people who consider it in their best self-interest to cooperate with one another. To create these social groups there doesn't necessarily have to be trust for there to be cooperation: self-interests and contracts can compensate for the absence of trust and make it possible to set up organizations that work for a common goal. Groups founded on self-interest can be created in any moment and their creation does not necessarily depend on cultural factors. Nonetheless, the most efficient organizations are based not only on norms and rules but on shared values as well. Social norms and values such as loyalty, honesty, reliability and, consequently, trust between people must be developed and accepted. This set of norms and values leads to the creation of social capital.

Robert Putnam defines social capital as the set of characteristics of social organizations, such as connections between individuals and norms of reciprocity and trustworthiness, that facilitate coordination and cooperation for mutual benefit. Rules and relationships allow people to coordinate their actions in order to achieve personal aims within a broader social context.

How can we identify social capital? Social capital can be found where there are social aggregations and, therefore, a certain quantity and quality of interaction. According to Robert Axelrod, social capital is incorporated in the concept of interaction and is a prerequisite for economic and social development. Social capital encourages reciprocity and increases the sense of trust among the members of a group. In a group where there are strong social interactions, negative behaviours, such as opportunistic and selfish behaviours, tend to be reduced. Where there is social capital, individual objectives can be integrated with social objectives, bringing together "I" with the broader "We".[113]

Whereas physical and human capital are more tangible and measurable, social capital is a resource that is born out of trust and is based on connections between people. Cultural mechanisms are used to create and diffuse social capital. It is not based only on the behaviour of individuals or on single values, but rather on the values of an entire group. Furthermore, though it can be difficult to create social capital, it is also more difficult to damage or destroy since it is founded on habits and ethical norms.

What relationship is there between social capital and organizations? One of the social roles of organizations is to facilitate the creation of relationships and, consequently, interpersonal interactions that can lead to the creation of social capital. Traditional organizations are vehicles for the creation and maintenance of social capital and exploiting the advantages it offers. The relationships between people make it possible to exploit, increase and renew social capital. New organizations seem to be heading towards a virtual and temporary way of working. However, if taken to an extreme, this could lead to potentially negative effects, such as individualism and isolation. The isolation created in a virtual organization could lead to a weakening or loss of important relationships. An increase in individualism might work against the development of social capital and the success of an organizational model based on trust.

Digital technologies make it possible to connect people and exchange information more easily and quickly. However, the downside of this is a loss of human contact between people. Therefore, we should ask ourselves which type of organization does a better job of generating and preserving social capital in terms of reciprocity, trust, collaboration and social identity. Though the answer to this question might at first appear to be traditional organizations, the success of the open source community seems to provide us with a different answer. The lack of formal rules and norms in the open source community would seem to indicate a significant loss of social capital. Nonetheless, other qualities, such as trust, giving and collaboration, are exalted. Therefore, it is possible to maintain and develop social capital in the context of virtual and temporary organizations so long as the new organizations are able to create and exploit social capital in new ways.

Our comparison between a traditional organizational model and the characteristics of the open source community highlighted a certain dichotomy between these two organizational approaches. However, the analysis was based on aspects that typically characterize traditional organizations. When we tried to identify these aspects in the context of the open source community, we found that they were either very different from or the antithesis of the same aspects in a traditional organization. What we must now ask ourselves is whether our analysis of the open source community should be based on traditional frameworks or whether we should look for new paradigms to interpret the open source phenomenon. In the next chapter, we will analyze the open source community using the complex adaptive systems theory.

Chapter 9

Open Source as a Complex Adaptive System

As we have seen in this book so far, the open source phenomenon does not follow the "rules" of commercial software development. The open source community has turned the concept of copyright upside down and created a new way of developing software and organizing work. These changes make it difficult, if not impossible, to analyze the open source phenomenon using consolidated frameworks. We need to look beyond these frameworks to find new concepts and theories that can explain this phenomenon. As we will see in this chapter, studies on complexity and complex systems offer a new framework for interpreting this unique form of organization that, regardless of the fact that it is seeminly chaotic, manages to produce significant results.

9.1 Complexity and Complex Systems

The concept of complexity has evolved over time and in some ways has followed the evolution of technology. If we take a look at the main steps in the evolution of technology, we can see that they correspond to the way our interpretation of complexity has evolved over time. The four main steps in the evolution of technologies and systems are: mechanical, information, communication, and biological technologies and systems.

The aim of mechanical technologies and systems was to reduce the physical effort required and substitute machines for man's physical functions. To do this industries developed more and more sophisticated levels of mechanization. The concept of complexity was based on the concept of mechanical machines.

Information technologies and systems were developed to elaborate information and substitute man in the functions of controlling and managing a system. The complexity framework that characterized this step was based on computer systems.

Communication technologies and systems for transmitting information introduced another characteristic of systems: connectivity. Network technologies and the Internet in particular made this evolutionary step possible. Networks allow the various users in the network to interact regardless of place and time. In this case, the network introduces a new complexity framework.

Biological technologies and systems bring together the knowledge of natural systems and that of technological systems. The best way to describe these systems is to use the concept of evolution. In this context, the behaviour of systems and the results they can produce are not completely predictable. This leads to yet another concept of complexity which is typical of biological systems.

This evolutionary path from the tightly-coupled systems of machines to the loosely-coupled systems of biological systems highlights how much the concept of complexity has evolved. This evolution has also influenced the way organizations have been analyzed. During the Industrial Revolution, the model of organizational design was based on the conceptual model of the machine. In this model, the concept of the hierarchical control of functions prevailed. The consequent approach was top-down thinking. Much of the organizational theory of the twentieth century was based on determinism, reductionism and equilibrium as key principles. If an organization is thought of as a machine, the organization is controlled by reducing complexity. The Information Revolution and development of networks have led to significant changes in this organizational model. In organizations today there is an ever-increasing connection between elements which are often extremely different from one another (computers, people, even smart objects). This has lead to phenomena which cannot be planned according to a top-down logic, but, on the contrary, "emerge" from interactions between elements and, therefore, "from the bottom". Consequently, the most suitable approach for analyzing these phenomena is bottom-up thinking.

If, in the past, the world could be represented as a machine, today it is represented as a network and gradually even more so as an eco-system. Internet, for example, can be considered not only a technological infrastructure and social habit, but also a new way of thinking related to the concepts of freedom of access and diffusion of knowledge.

As complexity has increased, it has become more and more difficult to describe and control systems using formal models. The difficulty in developing formal models is a function of the complexity of the relationships and interactions between the elements of the system itself with the consequent unpredictability of the results.

One of the characteristics of complex systems is *emergence*, i.e. the emergence of new states in a system which have new capabilities and offer new evolutionary possibilities. The very nature of emergence makes it difficult to foresee what the new states of the system will be since it is not always possible to extrapolate the new system properties from the existing system components. Nonetheless, one of the most interesting and significant aspects of the approach to complex systems is not the search for methods to limit their complexity, but, on the contrary, the exploitation of the complexity itself.[114]

The growth of the internet has led to the development of many types of on-line communities whose aims vary significantly. In particular, the open source community is unique because it develops something concrete, i.e. software products. The many communities working together to produce open source software offer new stimuli for research in the context of complexity theory. This is because the interactions between the various members are unpredictable as are the results of these interactions. Nonetheless, the organization works and the community develops quality products. These are examples of emergent characteristics of this community. By identifying the characteristics of a complex system present in the open source community, we can better understand how it works and see it as a new organizational model. Before doing this, it might be helpful to better understand exactly what complex adaptive systems are.

9.2 What are Complex Adaptive Systems?

A *complex system* is made up of a heterogenous group of inter-related elements. Some of these elements can be defined as *agents*, which can be defined as elements that have the ability to interact with each other and with their environment. Agents have three main characteristics: position, influence and memory. Position regards the space they work in, influence the set of behaviours that influence the system they work in, and memory their past experience, which allows them to make decisions regarding strategies to be adopted in the present and future. A strategy is the way in which agents pursue their own goals, interact with each other and react to stimuli from the environment. Strategies are selected using certain criteria or *measures of success* to evaluate their validity.[115]

An efficient strategy tends to be followed by many agents who then create a *population of agents* following the same strategy and using similar behaviours. The strategy determines the evolution of the system. Nonetheless, the lack of coordination and of a central authority in complex systems gives each agent the freedom to have and develop his/her own local and personal vision of the system. Even if the direction is suggested by the strategy, this does not impede some agents from following paths that are alternative, independent or even completely different from the direction followed by the majority of agents in the popoulation.

A system is said to be complex and adaptive when the agents have the possibility to constantly adapt their actions in response to the environment and the behavior of the other agents. For this reason the possibility to transfer information from one agent to another is particularly important in complex systems. This possibility depends on connectivity. A system is connected when each agent in the system can be reached by any other agent in the system. The greater the connectivity in a system is, the more possibilities there are to transfer information and, therefore, to increase the reciprocal influence between the agents in the system. The high level of connectivity that characterizes complex adaptive systems makes it possible to create a dynamic network of agents who are constantly communicating and interacting.[116]

The interaction between the agents leads the system to take on some *emergent properties*. These properties are not present in any one agent. The word "emergent" means that the properties of the system "emerge" from the interaction between the agents and are not dictated by a central authority. The emergent properties can lead the system towards new evolutions which cannot be foreseen. Therefore, a structured and predefined organization cannot work. Nonetheless, this does not mean that there is no organization. In fact, in a complex adaptive system, there are three process that determine the evolution of the system. These processes are variation, interaction and selection and are described in the following sections.

9.3 The Key Processes in Complex Adaptive Systems

The three key processes that determine the evolution of a complex adaptive system are variation, interaction and selection (Axelrod e Cohen, 1999). In every system, at any time, there is a certain degree of variety, which can be defined as the set of differences and alternatives that characterize both the agents and their strategies. Variety is the result of a process of variation, i.e. mutation of the set of alternatives. Variation determines the number of possible alternatives in the system. Interaction is a set of relationships and reciprocal influences that exist between agents and their strategies and the way in which these influences are exercised. Interactions are neither random nor can they be traced back to a completely predictable system. The quantity and quality of the interactions determine the dynamics of the system. Selection is the process of choosing, diffusing and eliminating the properties that characterize agents and their strategies. Therefore, it regards the ability the system has developed to identify which agents and strategies are to be chosen and thus diffused, and which, on the other hand, are to be eliminated. Consequently, selection determines the system's evolutionary directions.

9.3.1 Variation

Variation determines how many possible alternatives are present in a system. Variation makes it possible to consider a greater number of situations and, therefore, find a greater number of possible solutions. In other words, the greater the variation, the greater the complexity of the problems to be dealt with.

There can be both variation in agents and variation in strategies. An increase in variation is generally positive in both cases as it increases the diversity of the possible strategic options. By increasing the number of possible strategies, variation consequently offers the system the opportunity to evolve and adapt according to the dynamics of the surrounding environment. In other words, if the system has a large number of different agents and strategies, then it will probably be better able to adapt to new and not foreseeable situations.

Variation can be static, i.e. the result of pre-existing ideas or individual intuitions or actions, or dynamic, i.e. the result of the interaction between the agents in the system. In both cases variation, or continuous differentiation within a system, makes it possible to avoid the uniformity of the agents and their strategies. This is particularly important since uniformity can excessively limit the range of problems to be analyzed and solved.

Nonetheless, although variation is extremely useful and positive, it can inhibit the convergence of a system towards stable states in which appreciable results are produced. Excessive variation that is not accompanied by the possibility to converge towards desirable solutions can lead to a system in a precarious state of continuous research where anything is possible but nothing certain. Therefore, there is the need to find the right balance between variation and uniformity. Two possibile strategies can be adopted to do this. The first one, called exploration, is related to variation while the second one, called exploitation, is related to uniformity in a system.

Exploration is a long-run strategy whose objective it is to explore possible alternatives in order to increase heterogeneity and variety. Exploration consists in continuous research and learning. Though this strategy requires the system to invest in resources, the investments are repaid by greater guarantees of survival in the future.

The advantage of exploration is that it produces change and evolution. However, the drawback is that following this strategy alone can lead to instability, i.e. reduce the ability of a system to obtain satisfactory results over a short period of time. In fact, exploration limits a system's exploitation of the capabilities and strategies that already exist. An exploration strategy is, to a certain degree, the opposite of an exploitation strategy.

Exploiting the capabilities already present in a system is a short-run strategy aimed at guaranteeing the survival of the system in the present and obtaining the maximum benefit in the shortest time possible. Following only an exploitation strategy can also have negative effects, such as quickly making the system obsolete. Over time agents and strategies can use up their potential and lead the system, in the worst case possible, to extinction. This strategy can lead to the premature convergence of the system towards states which are not the best possible ones since it does not call for the necessary and sufficient exploration of the possible alternatives. While the advantage of this strategy is that it produces concrete results, the disadvantage is that it limits the system to obtaining these results in the present without considering the future.

To sum up, variation makes it possible to explore many possible alternatives, which means greater flexibility and faster evolution of the system. However, excessive variation can lead to a system away from its main objectives. In this case, the system is focused on finding many alternative paths without following one in particular.

9.3.2 Interaction

The second key process is interaction. Interaction guarantees the creation of relationships and, therefore, information flows between agents. The faster this flow of information is, the faster the dynamics of the system are. In other words, the faster the system can respond to events and variations that take place in the system. Therefore, interaction influences the dynamics of the system, and to a certain degree, its variety as well.

The interactions between agents shape the agents themselves and their strategies. Interaction offers the opportunity to evaluate and develop ideas and consequently diffuse strategies and behaviors. In other words, not only does it make it possible to create variety within populations, but it is also the premise for the processes of selection.

Two fundamental mechanisms produce interaction: proximity and activation.[117] The former refers to organizational interaction, the latter to process interaction.

Organizational interaction is related to the concept of proximity, which is the physical, virtual or conceptual position of an agent. Physical position describes exactly where agents are. Obviously, close physical proximity stimulates interaction. For example, two people who go to the same place at the same times will have many opportunities to interact. However, using new information and communication technologies such as the Internet, agents can interact without physical proximity. In this context, virtual position can substitute physical position. The third type of proximity is conceptual position. It is possible to represent some systems using a map of the conceptual space in which the agents define, organize and manage their interactions. The hierarchical structure of traditional organizations is an example of this type of map and an agent's conceptual space is defined by his/her position in the hierarchy. Projects and organizational culture can also create conceptual positions since they can draw agents together influencing their proximity. In the case of a project, proximity is created by shared objectives, and in the case of a value system or culture, proximity comes from shared ideas and values.

The other fundamental mechanism of interaction, activation, is related to processes. Product development processes bring agents together. For example, two agents whose activities take place one after another will have many more opportunities to interact than two agents whose activities are far apart in a process. In this case the interaction is differentiated and aimed at specific objectives. The development processes of products and the results of these processes create attraction. The frequency of development cycles also produces effects on interaction. The more frequent the cycles are, the more possibilities agents have to interact and gather new information internally, within the organization, and externally, through feedback from users. Activation can also limit the interactions and variety in a system because this mechanism is determined by the presence of regularity in a system. Therefore, both proximity and activation can limit the complexity of a system since they define privileged paths for interactions, or better, they define a structure in the system.

To conclude, interactions are partly caused by random events and partly caused by predictable ones that are determined by the structure of a system.

9.3.3 Selection

Selection is generally a mechanism that makes it possible to identify the best agents and/or behaviors, or in other words to promote the best characteristics. From the point of view of complex adaptive systems, selection is the ability to identify which agents and strategies are the best ones and to then decide which ones are to be diffused and which eliminated. Selection makes it possible to maintain, diffuse and eliminate characteristics and consequently influence the variety and diversity within the system. Therefore, selection influences interaction and especially variation. Selection also involves identifying the criteria that define success and updating these criteria.

There can be two levels of selection: the strategy level and the agent level. Strategy selection involves identifying which strategies are the best ones to meet the objectives of a system. Agent selection means identifying the winning agents without worrying about the strategies that make them successful. Strategy selection is costs less and has fewer consequences than agent selection. To select an agent means to create or duplicate a new agent starting from predefined models. This requires a long, costly and often impractical process because the entire set of characteristics of an agent must be reproduced and selected. On the contrary, since not all of the characteristics of the agents have to be changed when selecting and diffusing a strategy, this type of selection requires fewer resources and less effort, and is faster.

Nonetheless, when selecting a strategy, the context it comes from is lost. In other words, by isolating a strategy from its context could mean losing the effectiveness of the strategy itself. In this case, all of the synergies that might be the source of the success, i.e. the context, must be preserved. When it is not possible to identify these synergies and, therefore, not isolate and duplicate them outside of their context, it is better to select an agent.

Agents can actually be represented as a coordinated set of strategies. Therefore, when selecting an agent it is not necessary to understand the relationships between all of the agent's strategies. These relationships are selected as a block and, therefore, all of the synergies present in the context are maintained. In this case the selection is context preserving. In some systems, where outcomes are the result of complex relationships, preserving the context can help correctly conserve and diffuse the synergies that cannot be fully understood.

In addition to identifying the level of the selection, who and what is to be rewarded must be identified. In other words, how many and which criteria are used to identify successful agents and strategies must be defined. There are essentially two types of criteria for success: imitation and performance measures.

An agent or strategy is considered successful when it is present and repeated in large numbers within a population. Therefore, success is the result of a process of imitation that leads to the proliferation of some agents or strategies. This criteria is very simple in that all it requires is observing the system. However, imitation does not guarantee that the imitated behaviors are also the best ones.

Performance measures offer better guarantees that the agent or strategy selected is successful but they are more difficult to implement. Though performance measures are undoubtedly more reliable than imitation, it is not always possible to easily identify the best or most suitable measures. In fact, the since the measures are often defined by the agents themselves, they can be subjective and cause incongruities and conflicts. Therefore, it is very important to continuously search for and define objective measures that can be interpreted in an unequivocal way by agents inside or outside the system is very important.

A problem that both selection criteria share is determining the selection pressure. Selection pressure is the degree to which the successful elements are diffused, or the speed and breadth of the diffusion within the system. Pressure which is too high could lead to an exaggerated and premature selection of some elements. This could in turn quickly lead to the loss of variety within a population with all of the consequences this would have. On the contrary, pressure which is too low does not allow success elements to emerge. In other words, while variety is maintained, the system does not exploit the successful elements.

In complex systems selection criteria must be reviewed quite often combining long-run forecasts with results obtained in the short run. Frequently doing performance measurements makes it possible to update the measures used and, at the same time, identify or correct any wrong selections made. This allows the system to immediately react in a more efficient and flexible way to new situations and, therefore, to limit mistakes.

9.4 Open Source as a Complex Adaptive System

The open source community and its activities can be considered to have the characteristics of a system. The open source system is distinctive because it is neither controlled by a central authority that defines strategy and organization nor totally chaotic. It can be placed at an intermediate position between a planned system and a chaotic one.[118] In this position there are non-formalized rules which allow the system to produce significant results. The Complex Adaptive System theory can be used to better understand and analyze the open source system.[119]

The open source community can be considered an example of a complex adaptive system. It is made up of a population of heterogenous actors, each having his/her own role and self-defined strategies. In the open source community, the various roles are not rigidly assigned by a higher authority; on the contrary, each actor has the freedom to act and interact with the other actors in the system. Therefore, the actors in the open source community have the characteristics to be defined agents. They can influence the system by interacting with the rest of the community and are able to use their experience and memory to model their behavior in the present.

The definition of agent proposed by the complex adaptive system theory makes it possible to include free riders in this category as well. Free riders "are actors who take more than their fair share of the benefits or do not shoulder their fair share of the costs of their use of a resource, involvement in a project, etc.".[120] In the case of the open source community, the free riders are users who use open source products but do not directly contribute to the programming of new software. Nonetheless, users can stimulate the system, i.e. the community, through explicit and implicit feedback. Users are an integral part of the open source system since they participate in the processes of variation, interaction and selection and, by doing so, can influence the evolution of the system.

According to Axelrod and Cohen, the concept of complex adaptive system can be most easily related to applications which are long-term or diffused, require continuous innovation, need a lot of feedback in a short period of time or have a low risk of catastrophe. All of these characteristics can be found in open source products.

Long-term or diffused applications offer many opportunities for agents to come together. This leads to a critical mass which can activate significant processes of variation and interaction. In the case of software, examples of this type of applications are operating systems, network platforms, web servers, programming languages and all of the components and protocols which have created the standards of the Internet. Some spen source products are part of this category of long-term applications; they are usually platforms or common standards, e.g. Linux, Apache and PHP.

In the case of applications that require continuous innovation, i.e. in industries that are particularly dynamic, there is a signifcant need to explore new solutions. This is the case of software applications related to the Internet, such as web servers, protocols, browsers, etc. Since open source products are technologically advanced and innovative, they stimulate the creativity of the community and the continuous exploration of alternatives.

As far as applications which require a lot of feedback over a short period of time are concerned, significant advantages can be gained from the interaction between the agents in a development community. In the open source community, the users are considered to be the main source of inspiration for and evaluation of the quality of the products. The fact that products are available at a low cost makes it possible to obtain a significant quantity of information for free and to have the software undergo an extensive process of observation and checking based on daily use. The fact that the code is open and available to all makes it easier to carry out better measurements of product performance. This in turn gives agents a precise series of parameters they can use to objectively evaluate product performance and base their choices on.

Applications with a low risk of catastrophe are those for which the efforts committed to exploring alternatives should not put the survival of the entire system at risk. A system which manages to do this is dynamic and at the same time stable and, therefore, not at risk of implosion. The modular structure of open source products limits the effects that each activity can have on the entire product and makes it possible to avoid the propagation of any imperfections. The fact that the development process is carried out mainly by voluteers who work in parallel also lowers the risk of catastrophe. The results of each programmer's explorations are donated to the community in parallel. The failure of one or more exploration does not lead to the failure of the entire system, which nevertheless continues to survive since there are other agents involved in the development process. In fact, in open source no one agent is indispensable since nobody has total control over or responsibility for products and each activity is usually shared by a group of autonomous agents. Should any agent decide to stop carrying out his/her activities, he/she can easily and quickly be substituted regardless of the position he/she occupied.

The variation, interaction and selection processes described above can be identified in the open source community as well. Axelrod and Cohen consider open source mainly as an example of variation since it very much exploits the advantages gained from conserving diversity within a system. According to Axelrod and Cohen, one of the main dangers for a complex system is the extinction of a type of agent or strategy which reduces a system's diversity. Since the creation of a type requires resources and effort, its premature extinction should be avoided. A type which is not very successful in the present might have characteristics which could prove to be very important in the future. The open source community manages to preserve diversity by keeping track of the whole evolutionary process in order to be able to easily find anything that might be needed. Furthermore, usually no agent is excluded from participating in projects and this helps maintain a high level of variety.

We will now see that it is also possible to identify the interaction and selection processes in the open source community. Above all, we will take a look at how the close relationship that exists between these processes allows the open source community to efficiently and effectively exploit is own complexity.

Axelrod and Cohen identify a sequence in which the three processes take place. They consider variation to be a premise for the activation of different forms of interaction which, in turn, produce effects of selection within a system. However, it is possible to hypothesize that there are other sequences of variation, interaction and selection in the characteristics of the open source organization and development process discussed in Chapter 3, i.e. open participation, bottom-up organization, speed of development and parallel development. The benefit of each characteristic can be interpreted as one of the processes, but it is also possible to identify a negative effect, which can be interpreted as another process, and the actions taken to solve the problem can be interpreted as the remaining process (Figure 9.1).

The advantage of open participation, i.e. the free exploration of alternatives and flexibility of strategies, can be interpreted as **variation**. In the open source community, however, agents tend to work on development for long periods of time without making their solutions available. In this way, they do not stimulate the other agents in the community. This can be interpreted as a phenomenon of premature and highly subjective **selection**. In other words, this selection remains within the subjective evaluation of individual agents and does not benefit from the contribution of many different agents in terms of peer review. Furthermore, the agents are not solicited enough to offer new contributions to the development process.

The result of this is that the exploration process slows down, limiting the variety in the system. One solution to this problem is to increase the frequency with which software is released. Basically, the community makes a release each time there is a new feature, even if it is relatively insignificant, in order to motivate and involve the agents in the community. This action, seen from the point of view of complexity theory, has the effect of increasing the **interaction** between agents.

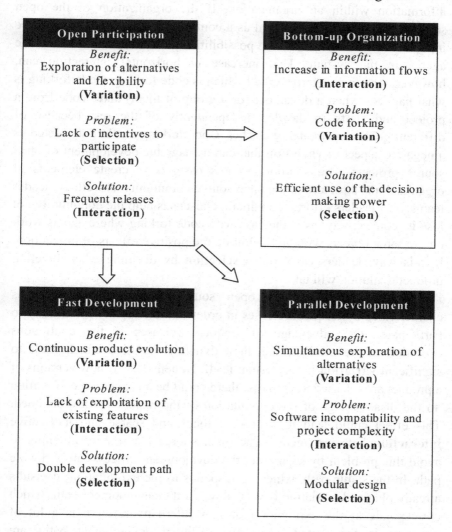

Figure 9.1 – Characteristics of a complex adaptive system in the open source community.

Another characteristic of the organizational structure of the open source community is decentralized decision-making power, i.e. the implementation of a bottom-up organization. As has often been noted, the advantage of decentralized power is an increase in the flow of information within an organization. If the organization of the open source community is interpreted as a complex system, this effect can be interpreted as an increase in the possibilities for **interaction** between the agents in the system. This increase in horizontal interaction can, however, lead to a negative effect which is code forking. Code forking is what happens when a developer (or a group of them) takes code from a project and starts to develop independently of the rest because of different goals or personality clashes. Code forking can be interpreted as a negative aspect of **variation** that can damage the development of open source projects. The solution, in this case, is to create elements of organizational structure in the open source community as well, i.e. leader teams. The leaders efforts to maintain consensus help the community not lose its connectivity, as is the case with code forking where agents work on the same objects without exploiting the positive effects of interaction. In this way, leaders carry out a **selection** by deciding what direction product evolution will take.

As we have seen, the open source development process is characterized by frequent releases in order to motivate the community to participate. The advantage of frequent releases is the continuous evolution of the products, i.e. their dynamic variation which leads to significant **variation** in the system itself. Nonetheless, if new versions of a product are released too rapidly, there could be an excess of exploration to the disadvantage of the exploitation of the results already obtained. This effect could lead to a lack of focus and scarse and ineffective **interaction** between agents. The open source community attempts to avoid this problem by separating the development process into a double path. In the stable path, which corresponds to the exploitation of results already obtained, variation is very slow. In the development path, which corresponds to the exploration of new alternatives, there is a lot of variation in the system. The two different development paths are managed through a process of **selection** in which contributions must be separated into two groups: on the stable path there are those which only need to be consolidated while on the development path there are those which need to be further developed.

Finally, there is the parallel development of products. The advantage of this is the possibility to explore a large number of different alternatives all at the same time. In other words, parallelism has the positive effect of **variation** regarding both the type of agents involved in the system and the strategies they pursue. Nonetheless, the parallel development of one product can also lead to excessive complexity and even the incompatibility between components and alternative product solutions. In fact, one single modification can have a significant impact on other parts of the product and the effect of the impact is unpredictable. This could be seen as a negative effect of the **interaction** between the elements in the system. The solution to the possible negative consequences is parallel development organized according to modular product planning. A precise definition of the modularity forces agents to make a **selection** of the objects they want to work on and at the same time limits the possible interferences with the activities of other agents.

In conclusion, in each of the functioning characteristics of the open source community it is possible to highlight the three fundamental processes of complex adaptive systems. Whereas in Axelrod and Cohen's variation-interaction-selection sequence, all the processes have positive effects on the system, we consider the possibility of other sequences characterized by the presence of a process having negative effects on the system. Finally, the solution to the problems caused by the negative effects of one of the processes can be interpreted as the effect of another one.

With the development of information networks, and the internet in particular, it has been observed that it is not necessarily possible to design and plan all phenomena that can be developed. In other words, the networks involve social structures that make these phenomena in some ways "emergent". This change has increased interest in an approach that interprets phenomena from the bottom up, i.e. from the network of relationships and interactions between actors. This led us to try and identify the characteristics of a complex system in the open source community.

After having presented the theory of complex adaptive systems, we interpreted the organization of open source community using this theory. The observations we have made in this chapter lead us to consider how this interpretation of open source can be extended to other contexts. Similar contexts could be all of those knowledge products that have characteristics similar to those of software. This extension could consider, for example, scientific research in general and highly innovative contexts in particular, such as bioinformatics and pharmaceutical research.

The open source community has taken advantage of its characteristics and its complexity in an attempt to offer a better solution and become a standard. The scope of the considerations we have made here could also be extended to analyze the strategies for the affirmation and diffusion of technological standards.

Finally, since the concept of complexity is very much related to social aspects, the theory of complex adaptive systems could be adapted to interpret networks and clusters. It should be clear that significant research must still be carried out to fully understand the rules, applicability and general usefulness of the concepts proposed by the complex adaptive systems theory.

Chapter 10

Developments

The concept of openness that is intrinsic to the open source phenomenon can be extended to other fields of application. The logic behind open source, taken in the broadest sense of peer production, could influence the production and diffusion not only of software, but of other knowledge products as well.

In 1999 Raymond predicted that the open source approach would influence fields other than software development: "I expect the open-source movement to have essentially won its point about software within three to five years (that is, by 2003–2005). Once that is accomplished, and the results have been manifest for a while, they will become part of the background culture of non-programmers. At *that* point it will become more appropriate to try to leverage open-source insights in wider domains".[121]

This chapter focuses on the extension of the concept of production and how it is influenced by the concepts of collaboration and openness. The concept of openness is being applied not only to processes, but to products as well in what is now commonly called open content. There are many web-based projects that gather, organize, distribute and/or produce open content to varying degrees. We will also take a look at the legal aspects of open content, i.e. how these various projects are guaranteeing that what they produce remains open. We will see how a concept that was originally applied only to software, i.e. copyleft, has been extended to many other fields where knowledge is produced.

10.1 Extension of the Concept of Openness

10.1.1 Peer-to-peer production

In the development of knowledge products, as is the case in scientific research, horizontal relationships, or peer relationships, are very important. Peer-to-peer interaction is a two-way interaction in which every player in a communication network has the same possibilities to send, receive, manage and control information. Peer-to-peer interaction makes it possible to create communities where players can share information, opinions and resources, and thus collaborate on the development and evolution of different projects. Peer-to-peer interaction is a new way of exchanging information and knowledge and, therefore, of developing projects.

In the open source phenomenon, the traditional concept of production has evolved into the new concept of peer production, or peer-to-peer (p2p) production. As we have already seen, software is a knowledge product whose development activities play a more important role than its production activities. Production is nothing more than reproducing at an irrelevant costs what has been developed. Therefore, when we speak about software we can use the word production to refer to the development process rather than to production in the strict sense of the word.

Peer production refers to a group of self-organized people who assign themselves goals and activities.[122] It is particularly suitable organization models where human resources are more important than any other type of resource. Peer production is based on the availability of a theoretically unlimited number of resources that can be obtained from a theoretically unlimited number of players. The unlimited nature of these resources makes it possible to increase the entire productive capacity of a system. The potential benefits that come from the possibility of being able to count on the collaboration and availability of different resources actually increase the size of the community.

In a "closed" production model, ownership and contracts are used to ensure the presence and access of resources for production. Turnover comes at a cost because it means having to adapt and renew human resources to the needs of production. On the contrary, in a peer-to-peer "open" production model, any person can autonomously join a project and human resources are brought together and used in a better and more flexible way.

The concept of openness can be integrated with the more general concept of collaboration. You can see this effect when you go on the internet to search for information. The world wide web is the best example of a global container created by the collaboration, more often than not for free, of millions of users. The value of the internet lies not as much in its being free of charge, but rather more so in its openness. This characteristic makes it possible to exploit a more or less unlimited potential of human resources.

10.1.2 Open content

Open content can be considered a conceptual model or a philosophy. The aim of this philosophy is to apply open source principles and strategies to various other types of contents and information that can be freely accessed on the world wide web. Users also have the possibility to modify the open content. This is based on the idea that giving peers the possibility to edit is the best way to improve the contents, and keep them updated as well. In other words, the aim of open content is to create and maintain a community of users and participants in order to obtain extensive collaboration for the development of single projects. "[T]he open content movement is beginning to stir for precisely the same reasons that launched the Free Software movement in the 1980s: the realization that a for-profit industry was about to lock up indispensable public knowledge and, in so doing, pose a grave threat to the advancement of knowledge and human welfare."[123]

Open content has become a social phenomenon that has created enough interest to promote technological innovation and cultural evolution. In Table 10.1 we can see some projects that successfully apply open source principles to other knowledge-related activities. The activities considered deal with collecting, organizing, accrediting, diffusing and producing knowledge. The complexity of these activities varies quite a lot from the simple activities of gathering and diffusing knowledge to the much more complex activities of producing contents and knowledge.

The main activities carried out in Amazon.com and the OpenCourseWare project are respectively the organization of knowledge and diffusion of open content. The Project Gutenberg and Wikipedia basically involves the collection of open content. Google, the Open Directory Project and Slashdot are examples of projects in which peer evaluation and accreditation are used to classify open content. The last two projects, the Nasa Clickworkers and Bioinformatics.org, are actually involved in producing knowledge.

Now we will take a closer look at the way these projects have been influenced by the open source logic.

Table 10.1 – Extension of the open source logic to other projects.
(■ = main activity; • = other important activity)

Activities / Projects	Knowledge Organization	Knowledge Diffusion	Peer Collection	Peer Accreditation	Peer Production
Amazon	■	•		•	
OpenCourseWare	•	■		•	
Gutenberg	•	•	■		
Wikipedia		•	■		•
Google	•	•		■	
Open Directory Project	•	•		■	
Slashdot	•	•		■	
NASA Clickworkers			•	•	■
Bioinformatics.Org			•	•	■

10.1.3 Knowledge organization

Amazon is the world's largest online retailer of books and other publications. The main activities at Amazon are organizing the information regarding the titles offered, evaluating and accrediting the publications, and distributing products to users. The main service offered is guiding the customer in the purchasing process through the use of tools that classify and search for contents. Basically Amazon may be used as a well organized library where users can browse for almost any type of book. Although Amazon is involved in knowledge organization, openness and collaboration do not characterize the services it offers.

Why, then, can we see Amazon as an extension, even if in a limited way, of an open logic? Amazon does actually have a system for attributing importance and accreditation to the publications it offers which is based on peer-to-peer mechanisms, i.e. peer-to-peer relevance. The system collects readers comments and memorizes what customers buy in order to produce feedback that can be used by future customers. In other words, by observing the behaviour of its own users and their needs, Amazon can help guide future customers towards the offers and services that might interest them more.

10.1.4 Knowledge diffusion

The OpenCourseWare (OCW) project was started by the Massachusetts Institute of Technology (MIT) with the aim of distributing a part of the material used in its university courses on the Internet. As stated in the OCW welcome page, the project is "a free and open educational resource for faculty, students, and self-learners around the world. OCW supports MIT's mission to advance knowledge and education, and serve the world in the 21st century."[124] OpenCourseWare does not distribute all of the knowledge contents offered in its courses, but rather only distributes teaching material, excluding textbooks and other material protected by copyright. The main activities involved in the project are organizing the teaching material and diffusing it via the internet. The creators of the project do not consider knowledge to be a private good, but rather a good that must be transferred and built up by involving students in the process.

The aim of the project is to help students develop their own cultural background in a more autonomous way.

The OpenCourseWare project was divided into three distinct stages. The first stage involved the experimentation of the pilot project, in which material from the first trial courses was published online. During this stage, the project's stakeholders were involved in evaluating the main technological aspects. The aim of the second stage of the project, which should last about two years, is to increase the amount of material available online. During this stage the material from about one hundred courses is expected to be published the web. Furthermore, the project foresees that some entire degree courses will be included in OCW in the future. The aim of the third and final stage, which is expected to last two years, is to complete the "process of opening" by including material from all of the courses offered at MIT (about 2000).

The project takes advantage of some of the mechanisms of the open source logic to improve the quality of the contents offered online. Even though access to the teaching material is controlled from a center, it is free and thus makes it possible to have a certain degree of peer review from the online community, which is made up of both experts and simple users. Through peer review the material distributed can be developed and checked, and then the feedback collected through the evaluation of the quality of the contents (peer evaluation) can be used to accredit the material.

Both the organization and diffusion of the contents are managed in a centralized way by the project staff. Nonetheless, the influence of the open source logic is a determining factor for the philosophy of the entire project. In fact, as is the case with open source software, OpenCourseWare guarantees free access to all the material on its web site. Freedom is considered the premise for creating knowledge and stimulating innovation and research.

OpenCourseWare seems to be a countertendency: while there is an ever-growing increase in the commercialization of educational activities based on the ideas of knowledge as a good and education as a product, the OCW project is based on sustainability, democracy and free access to knowledge. As Charles M. Vest, former President of MIT explains, "OpenCourseWare looks counter-intuitive in a market-driven world. It goes against the grain of current material values. But it really is consistent with what I believe is the best about MIT. It is innovative. It expresses our belief in the way education can be advanced by constantly widening access to information and by inspiring others to participate."[125] Not only is the OCW project sustainable from an economic point of view, but it makes it possible to exploit human capital in the best way possible and promote innovation and growth in a knowledge-based society.

10.1.5 Peer collection

The concepts of openness and collaboration can be found in Project Gutenberg and Wikipedia as they are involved in collecting and diffusing information and knowledge.

In 1971 Michael Hart started Project Gutenberg with the aim of creating a complete public domain digital library whose contents could be retrieved for free by users via the internet. The fundamental assumption at the heart of the project was the infinite reproducibility of digital products. In fact, the project logo states, "Fine Literature Digitally Re-Produced".[126] The project grew slowly during its first 20 years due to the limited diffusion of the internet outside academic and professional contexts. However, the expansion of the internet in the 90s helped the project grow exponentially.

The main activities of Project Gutenberg are collecting, putting into digital format, publishing and distributing non-specialist texts for free via the internet. The project's stakeholders are not professionals and researchers, but rather a vast community of simple enthusiasts and users in search of information. Contributors transform material not subject to copyright into digital format. This process is carried out in parallel thanks to the community of volunteer contributors (peer collection). The influence of the open source logic can be found in the collaboration involved in the collection process.

The evaluation of the contents published are influenced by peer review. In order to make this process effective, certain tools, such as forums and mailing lists, are needed. Project Gutenberg offers these tools to support the community of collaborators that do peer-based distributed proofreading. Distributed proofreading allows each member of the community to be involved in re-reading and correcting single pages. The efforts of many people are spread out making it possible to rebuild entire books, even long ones, by simply putting together each member's contributions.

Possibly the greatest impact of Project Gutenberg is a social one. The diffusion of knowledge can be considered one of the best uses, from a social point of view, of the internet. Michael Hart, founder of Project Gutenberg, believes that the project can be one way of fighting illiteracy and ignorance for it offers everyone access to free information, education, and literacy.

Another example of an application of the concept of peer collection is the Wikipedia project. The aim of this project is to create a free, open encyclopedia. The main activities involve collecting a significant amount of information and creating an effective, efficient and reliable resource. The contributions are collected via the internet. Wikipedia is basically a self-built encyclopedia in that anyone can contribute new information or edit existing information. The welcome page on the Wikipedia.org website states: "Wikipedia is an encyclopedia written *collaboratively* by its readers. The site is a Wiki, meaning that anyone, including *you*, can edit any article right now by clicking on the edit this page link that appears at the top of every Wikipedia article." Wikipedia goes one step further than the Project Gutenberg in the sense that collaboration in this case can lead to the production of new open content.

The members of the Wikipedia community share a set of values that make it possible to guide the behaviour of the community itself. One of the main problems is maintaining the right amount of objectivity and impartiality in developing and editing contents. The material collected is organized and diffused according to a set of rules and conventions authors must agree to follow (naming conventions). For example, Wikipedia uses a section, called "talk pages", where any changes made to contents collected are discussed in a democratic way. This makes it possible to involve a large part of the community in this delicate activity. Contributors can also discuss and modify the conventions. In this community, the participation and discussion of members have a greater value than the formal rules.

The dynamic nature of the Wikipedia community very much resembles the open source community where reputation, discussion and debate are more important than formal rules. Both communities are also made up of a set of heterogeneous, voluntary, independent contributors spread out all over the world. These people, though motivated by different reasons, do not share formalized rules and behaviours, but rather support the culture of collaboration and openness with the aim of diffusing impartial, quality knowledge.

10.1.6 Peer accreditation

As the amount of information available on the internet has increased, it has become necessary to develop more and more innovative and effective search engines. A search can give a user a large amount of information, much of which may be useless for that particular user. In order to make it easier for users to find what they are looking for, search engines need to evaluate and accredit information. Initially search engines used automatic technologies and search tools. Clearly, however, these technologies are limited. Companies that offer search services have begun to value the human factor by developing peer accreditation and peer relevance techniques that are more reliable than evaluation tools based exclusively on automatic algorithms. We will now take a look at a few projects that have adopted and made use of these concepts to varying degrees.

Google is essentially a search engine that uses algorithms to evaluate and classify web pages according to various factors. One of the most important algorithms is called PageRank. The algorithm assigns the importance of a page based on how many times a given page is found as a link in other pages. PageRank also considers the importance of the pages where the links are found. In this way, the algorithm indirectly collects the evaluation of many users since the number of times a site is linked to can be considered an implicit attribution of relevance to the site. In other words, the search engine can classify and list the pages in order of an attributed relevance (peer relevance). Even though the search engine is an automatic tool, it has clearly been designed to indirectly take advantage of the human factor as well.

Other projects judge relevance based on opinions given directly by users. This is how the Open Directory project works. The aim of this project is to collect and catalogue web pages. Opinions are not collected by using algorithms, but rather by the direct evaluation of a global community of volunteer editors. As the number of web sites continues to grow, human intervention is needed to guarantee that the web directories are updated. The number of editors at commercial directory sites is limited whereas the number of potential volunteer editors is unlimited. At present Open Directory "...powers the core directory services for the Web's largest and most popular search engines and portals, including Netscape Search, AOL Search, Google, Lycos [...] and hundreds of others".[127]

Another example is the Slashdot project. Started in 1997, the aim of the project is to collect news and comments regarding the Internet, hardware and software technologies and scientific developments in the ICT industry, or as the web site says: "News for nerds. Stuff that matters".[128] Slashdot uses a complex system for selecting and accrediting material and for defining roles and responsibilities to the people involved in the project.

A part of the Slashdot community is made up of moderators who evaluate every single comment using a series of parameters to consider aspects such as how original or up-to-date contents are. In this way users can choose to not read material whose evaluation has not reached a certain level. The moderators are chosen by the community from among the users that have been involved in the Slashdot project for a long time, i.e. those that have a solid reputation within the community. The role of moderator is subject to continuous evaluation by the community. There is a peer review accreditation mechanism, called meta-moderation, that users can use to express their opinions on how moderators are working and limit their power should they behave inappropriately. The combination of moderation and meta-moderation allow Slashdot to guarantee the presence of a solid and reliable infrastructure based on so-called real-time peer review. Slashdot uses a model for defining roles and responsibilities that is in many ways similar to the way this process takes place in the open source community.

10.1.7 Peer production

As we have already seen, the open source logic and peer production can influence the production not only of software but of other knowledge products as well. We will now briefly describe two projects that are involved in producing specialist scientific knowledge. The first one, NASA Clickworkers, is a limited project whereas the second one, Bioinformatics.org, is much larger and is influencing the development of the entire scientific discipline after which it is named.

The aim of NASA Clickworkers is to study the possibility of using collaboration mechanisms in scientific research. Public volunteers called clickworkers are asked to find and communicate information regarding craters on the surface of the planet Mars. The aim of this experiment is to evaluate whether contributions coming from a large number of voluntary users can actually substitute the work of scientists and researchers in the simpler and more repetitive activities. If so, researchers could dedicate their time to more creative and important work.

There are obviously errors and redundancies, but an analysis of the quality of the results on average has led to the conclusion that the contributions obtained from a large number of Clickworkers is not less correct than the contribution of an expert researcher. In other words, the project confirmed the value of collaboration and peer review and, more importantly, the possibility of successfully distributing some activities involving research and knowledge production (peer production).

An even more significant example of peer production is Bioinformatics.org, a project that was founded for the development of technologies, tools and knowledge in the field of bioinformatics. The amount of data available for scientific research has increased exponentially in recent years. At the same time new technologies and computational tools have made it possible to link scientific research in biology and informatics. Bioinformatics.org uses information systems to analyze large quantities of data. One famous example of this type of application is the genome project which is aimed at finding the sequences of the human genome. Bioinformatics.org is a non-profit international organization founded in 1998 and hosted by the University of Massachusetts Lowell. Bioinformatics.org provides the resources needed for the research, development and diffusion of bioinformatics knowledge. The organization promotes the concepts of freedom and openness to diffuse the use of these resources.

The project maintains that the "open" model is the tool needed to satisfy the needs of scientific research.

> We [Bioinformatics.org] were inspired by the free and Open Source software movements and their ideology that information should be kept free. Oddly, these movements are based on the impression that the scientific community is completely open and a place where ideas are shared freely. We know this to be a false impression, but Bioinformatics.org is an attempt to live up to it, not to correct it.[129]

In order to identify and solve errors and define new directions and approaches to developing research projects, researchers have to be able to communicate and collaborate. In an open context there are fewer barriers to accessing the competences needed to carry out research. Bioinformatics.org promotes research projects whose results are accessible and distributed for free. Openness also promotes education and continuous learning for students and researchers.

The project developed thanks to the diffusion of the Internet and the development of distributed network applications. By using the Internet it is possible to solve problems in bioinformatics that require significant calculation capabilities and are most likely not available in just one laboratory.

The dispersion of researchers all over the world and the ever-increasing number of software packages used has required the project to make integration efforts. Research is often slowed down by the need to exchange information collected in very different formats that are sometimes incompatible. Therefore, another aim of the project is to identify and develop standards that make it easier to exchange and use information.

Bioinformatics.org shows that the open source logic can be applied to contexts other than software and that peer production to produce scientific knowledge can be effective.

10.2 Copyleft Applied to Non-Software Products

So far in this chapter we have considered web-based projects that have adopted various aspects of the fundamental characteristics of the open source community: collaboration and peer-to-peer evaluation, accreditation, production, etc. These concepts regard the interactions between members of a community, but what about the open content these communities collect, organize and/or produce and make available on the Internet? How are intellectual property rights being applied to this open content or how can they be applied?

The internet is basically nothing more than a container of knowledge and information. As a system, the internet can be broken down into three layers, each of which can be either free or controlled: a physical layer, a code layer and a content layer.[130] The physical layer includes the wires, computer or hardware that actually make up the system. The code layer is the logistical nature of the internet and consists of the hardware, protocols and software that make up the architecture of the network. The third layer is the content layer and includes all of the content found on the internet from facts and information to audio files and free software. While the physical layer is made up of products that are all owned or controlled by someone, the code layer is free. The content layer, however, is made up of both controlled and free resources. Much debate is taking place today on what should or should not be free and how to protect what is free and keep it free.

The solutions the open source community and Free Software Foundation came up with to protect free software and keep it open can be applied and are being applied to products other than software. One of these solutions is copyleft which, as we have already seen in Chapter 2, protects the origin of the software, i.e. it requires that any derivative works from a given product maintain the same terms as the license that protected the original product (*share and share alike*).

The purpose of copyright is to protect literary, scientific and artistic works such as books and music. When software began to be considered a commercial product and the source code original expression, copyright laws were applied to software to prevent copying or modifying the code. Copyleft was then created to oppose the limitations imposed by copyright and guarantee the possibility to copy, modify and distribute source code. It seems only natural, then, that there be the possibility to apply copyleft not only to software but to the literary, scientific and artistic works copyright has always been applied to.

One of the first steps taken to apply copyleft to non-software products was the application of the General Public License, originally created for software, to the documentation that comes with any software product. As Richard Stallman, founder of the Free Software Foundation, wrote in 1990, "[t]he biggest deficiency in free operating systems is not in the software - it is the lack of good free manuals that we can include in these systems."[131] According to Stallman, it was important not only to guarantee the redistribution of the manuals in electronic or paper format, but to allow users the possibility to make changes as well. In other words, all of the basic concepts of copyleft should be applied to software documentation as well. In fact, the need to copyleft these sorts of materials led the Free Software Foundation to release the first version of the "GNU Free Documentation License" in 2000. According to the official GNU project website, the GFDL "…is a form of copyleft intended for use on a manual, textbook or other document to assure everyone the effective freedom to copy and redistribute it, with or without modifications, either commercially or noncommercially."[132]

The GFDL was the practical result of a more general trend that was taking place in many knowledge fields. This trend was, as we have already seen, the desire not only of software programmers, but of authors, artists and scientists, to create open content that could be freed up of the limitations imposed by copyright and at the same time and be protected with copyleft. Two of the most impressive examples of the realization of these ideas are the Creative Commons project and the Public Library of Science (PLoS) project. The former is a project aimed at diffusing knowledge and creativity in general while the latter is, as can be seen by the name, aimed specifically at diffusing scientific knowledge. We will now take a look at these two projects, and mention a few others, in order to see how copyleft is being applied to other knowledge products.

10.2.1 Creative Commons

In 2001, Lawrence Lessig founded Creative Commons, a not-for-profit organization devoted to creating a web space where creative work can be placed, shared and legally built on by others. The aim of the organization's first, and possibly most important project, which was to develop a set of copyright licenses free for public use called the Creative Commons Public Licenses (released in December 2002). "Creative" because the licenses "...are not designed for software, but rather for other kinds of creative works: websites, scholarship, music, film, photography, literature, courseware, etc.".[133] "Commons" because the aim of the organization is to create a space and a community where artists can freely share their work. As explained in the project's web site, "...Creative Commons has developed a Web application that helps people dedicate their creative works to the public domain - or retain their copyright while licensing them as free for certain uses, on certain conditions"[134]. This underlines the fact that while the project promotes donating creative works to the public domain where the work receives no protection, it recognizes the fact that freedom of expression also has the right to be protected by licenses other than copyright. The licenses do not oppose copyright, but rather attempt to change some of the limitations imposed by copyright in order to adapt them to the new context of open content.

Whereas copyright guarantees "all rights reserved", and Public Domain "no rights reserved", Creative Commons Public Licenses offer "some rights reserved". In other words, a work protected by a CCPL is available to everyone but under certain conditions chosen by the author. The 11 licenses available are various combinations of four basic conditions, which are:

- *Attribution*: credit must always be given to the original author of the work, regardless of how the work is modified or copied, if a derivative work is made, etc.
- *Noncommercial*: the work cannot be used for commercial uses
- *No Derivative Works*: the work can be copied, distributed or performed only in its original form and no derivative works can be made based on the work

- *Share Alike*: derivative works can only be distributed under a license identical to the license that governs the original work.

Authors can choose the license with the combination of conditions that best suits their needs. However, there are baseline rights and restrictions that apply to all of the licenses. For example, every license allows others to copy the work, distribute it, display or perform it publicly, make digital public performances of it, and change the format of the work. All of these basic restrictions adhere to the concept of free access in the open source logic.

The standard Creative Commons licenses can be applied to Audio, Images, Video, Text and Education materials. In addition to these standard CCPLs, Creative Commons has also developed two licenses specifically for sampling and music sharing. Creative Commons developed its Sampling license together with Negativland, an experimental music and art collective that uses "found sounds" and musical samples to make new original collage art or "mash-ups". Creative Commons and Negativland maintain that there is a significant difference between piracy and bootlegging, and sampling and collage because the latter two involve the creative transformation of an original work. Whereas copyright can be justified in the case of bootlegging, Creative Commons feels it is inappropriately used to prohibit sampling and collage. Once again, the logic behind the Sampling License is to give artists the freedom to create and share while respecting the integrity of each other's work. This license can also be applied to photography, images, film or any other creative work protected by copyright. The Music Sharing license is for artists who want fans to be able to legally download and share their music and at the same time protect their music from commercial use and remixing.

In order to make the Creative Commons Public Licenses user-friendly and at the same time practical and effective, they are expressed in three ways: "Human Readable Common Deed", "Lawyer Readable Legal Code" and "Machine Readable Digital Code". The first format is a sort of summary of the terms of the license that can be easily understood. The Legal Code is written in legal language and can serve as the official text in case of any legal problems. The electronic version, or Digital Code, allows search engines and other applications to identify the work and how it is licensed. Creative Commons suggests that authors who have used CCPLs for their works include a button on their page with the Creative Commons logo (a double "c" in a circle, rather than copyright's one single "c" in a circle) which also serves as a link to the Common Deed of the license that has been chosen so that users can, if necessary, access the Legal Code. The CCPLs work around what many artists and intellectuals consider to be the drawbacks to copyright. At the same time, by guaranteeing certain rights, these licenses stimulate sharing and collaboration within a community of users. Though the GNU Public License and the Open Source Definition open source licenses are specifically intended for software, they share the basic concepts of freedom and openness with Creative Commons.

Creative Commons has also started some other projects. One is icommons, or international commons. The aim of icommons is to promote the creation of organizations similar to Creative Commons in other countries and coordinate their activities. Although other countries might share the same concepts and values, the Creative Commons licenses are, to a certain degree, based on the United States Copyright Act. Therefore, the project involves adapting the CCPLs to the laws in other countries and then producing a translated version of at least the Legal Code. Jurisdiction-specific licenses have already been created for Brazil, Finland, Germany, Japan and the Netherlands and are being worked on for several other countries.

Another interesting project is "Founders' Copyright". This project is a sort of compromise for those who do not want to give up copyright, but recognize that the 70+ years of copyright in the USA might be a bit excessive. The framers who wrote the United States Constitution and the first copyright law (1790) gave authors a monopoly right of 14 years over their works with the possibility of renewing the copyright only one time for another 14 years. The maximum time, therefore, that America's founding fathers established for the duration of copyright was 28 years. The aim of the Founders' Copyright project is to give authors the possibility to choose to return to the 14 (maximum 28) year copyright. Authors can sign a symbolic, but legally valid, contract with Creative Commons that will guarantee that their work will become part of the public domain after 14 or 28 years. Authors sell the copyright protecting their work to Creative Commons for $1.00. Creative Commons then gives the authors an exclusive license to their works for 14 (or 28) years. In return, during the years the works are protected by copyright, Creative Commons will list them under the Founders' Copyright, along with the projected public domain liberation date, in an online registry. In this way, the authors get visibility and publicity through being a part of a large digital archive of artistic works.

One other project worth mentioning is the development of the Science Commons. The aim of this project is "...to encourage scientific innovation by making it easier for scientists, universities, and industries to use literature, data, and other scientific intellectual property and to share their knowledge with others."[135] It is a return to the basic principles of scientific research for which scientific fact, data and research must be shared and open. Technology can promote this process of sharing but intellectual property law can hinder it. As with all other Creative Commons licenses, the aim is to work within copyright and patent law to develop legal mechanisms that promote knowledge sharing.

10.2.2 Public Library of Science (PloS)

The diffusion of scientific research is a fundamental part of scientific progress and innovation. According to the Public Library of Science, the project discussed in this section, "[i]mmediate unrestricted access to scientific ideas, methods, results, and conclusions will speed the progress of science and medicine, and will more directly bring the benefits of research to the public."[136] Many scientists believe that the application of copyright to scientific findings obstructs the progress of science. Copyleft applied to scientific information is proving to be a solution to the current limits placed on scientific publications by copyright laws.

Since the beginning of the 1990s various academics, researchers and institutions have made attempts at creating free-access libraries for scientific literature (arXiv.org, PubMed Central) but these initiatives have not always been welcomed by scientific publishers and, consequently, in the end have not succeeded in creating significant databases. In 2000, a coalition of research scientists dedicated to making scientific and medical literature a free public resource founded the Public

Library of Science. After unsuccessfully calling on scientific publishers to make the primary research articles they publish available through online public libraries, in the summer of 2001 this group of scientists decided that PLoS would have to make its own journals. In October 2003, PLoS published the first issue of *PLoS Biology* online and in print. Given the immediate success of the journal, PLoS has made plans to publish journals in other fields such as Medicine, Physics and Chemistry. According to the website, "These journals will not only provide a high-quality and high-profile venue for important discoveries in science and medicine, but they will provide a model for open-access publication and a catalyst for change in the publication industry."[137] The project has caught the attention of numerous academic institutions and research centers bringing the issue of scientific publications and copyleft into an important debate.

The core principles of PLoS highlight the relationship between this project and the open source logic. The first core principle is unrestricted open access for use and reproduction provided the original work is cited. The concept of coordination can be found in the principles of cooperation, community engagement and internationalism which highlight the commitment to work collectively, in a decentralized way, welcoming anyone who believes in the initiative into the community. Finally, in order to guarantee open access, PLoS uses the Creative Commons Attribution License, the same one that covers the Creative Commons website.

10.2.3 Other projects

Whereas Creative Commons developed copyleft licenses for any type of creative work, there are several other projects like PLoS which are more field-specific.

Before Creative Commons was founded, there was the Open Content project which was dedicated to creating open content. It released two licenses specifically for literary works: the Open Content License in 1998 and the Open Publication License in 1999. Though the Open Publication License, which better respects the copyleft model, was primarily designed for academics, it can also be adapted to the needs of artists or other creators of content. This project was eventually absorbed by the Creative Commons organization.

Art Libre is a French project dedicated to diffusing the copyleft attitude and applying it to all creative works. The project's "Licence Art Libre", "Free Art License" in English, respects all of the basic principles of copyleft and has some characteristics that cannot be found in other copyleft licenses. For example, this license indicates the duration of the license, sub-licensing and the law applicable to the license, i.e. French Law. The preamble clearly states that the basic aim of the license is "...to promote and protect artistic practice freed from the rules of the market economy."[138] This license is the only one that has been developed in a completely European context.

In the field of law, some academics at Harvard University wanted to apply the spirit of sharing to legal issues. They started a project called Open Law not only to diffuse content, but more importantly to find solutions to legal problems in a collaborative effort. The site organizers present cases of interest and then ask users, both lawyers and non-lawyers, to contribute their ideas, comments and suggestions to help develop arguments, draft pleadings, and edit briefs. As stated in the project's web site, "Building on the model of open source software, we are working from the hypothesis that an open development process best harnesses the distributed resources of the Internet community. By using the Internet, we hope to enable the public interest to speak as loudly as the interests of corporations."[139] The cases presented in the forum deal with issues such as open access, copyright versus copyleft, etc.

One more project worth mentioning is the Electronic Frontier Foundation. The slogan gives a very good idea of the what this project is all about: "Defending Freedom in the Digital World". The Electronic Frontier Foundation is a nonprofit group of lawyers, volunteers and visionaries who work together to protect and defend digital rights. In addition to providing a database of information about digital rights on its website, the organization sponsors legal cases to protect users' online civil liberties, supports innovations in technology, and provides free advice for members of the online community. Particular attention is given to peer-to-peer (P2P) technologies. The Electronic Frontier Foundation maintains that the music industry has wrongly attacked the technologies rather than the users who violate copyrights. According to the website, "[p]eer-to-peer technology is a wonderful tool for the mass distribution of all sorts of content. The Electronic Frontier Foundation believes that, in its zeal to stop illegal trading of copyrighted songs online, the music industry will cause significant damage to the developers of this new technology."[140] One of the initiatives to support sharing original music was the release of the Open Audio License (OAL) version 1.0 and the designation of the Creative Commons Attribution Share-Alike license as version 2.0 of the Open Audio License. The Electronic Frontier Foundation made this switch because the Creative Commons license shares the same principles as version 1.0 of the Open Audio License but offers consistency in licensing and the CC Digital Code facilitates sharing and combining works.

10.3 Conclusions and Open Questions

My aim in writing this book was to present the open source phenomenon from different points of view. In order to fully understand this phenomenon, many different aspects, i.e. technical, economic, social and political aspects, must be taken into consideration. These must be studied not only to understand the open source community but to understand what influence it has had and may have beyond the software development community.

The structure of the open source development community and the interpretation of the various roles and interactions between the members of this community will continue to be one of the main focuses of research in this context. How will the composition of the development community and the internal interactions evolve? What new organizational problems will the community have to face as new players join the community, especially if we consider the involvement of large firms and public institutions? Might the involvement of these players change or even undermine the characteristics of the open source community?

It might also be useful to evaluate the ethical, social, technical and economic motivations that support the community since these motivations could undergo significant changes in the future. Will reputation capital continue to be, and to what degree will it be, the main motivating factor for participating in the open source community?

Can the way the open source community develops software can be considered a model for software development? To answer this question, it will be necessary to identify some parameters and measures to evaluate the quality of the activities and results of open source development.

The open source logic could also influence the evolution of innovation models. The way this community works demonstrates the importance of factors such as involving users in the product definition and development processes, generating innovative ideas from the outside. It also shows the effectiveness of new forms of leadership and a more open management of information flows.[141]

The open source phenomenon will probably continue to have an impact on business strategies. It is interesting to observe how the open source phenomenon has influenced and will continue to influence the behaviour of other economic players, especially as far as copyright and intellectual property rights are concerned. This phenomenon seems to question the principles and practices of intellectual property protection. Does accepting open source philosophy necessarily mean opposing property rights and copyright? How can firms deal with this problem? How can a company become involved in the open source community and at the same time continue to make a profit?

Even if it is difficult to identify an organizational model in the traditional sense of the word in the open source community, the way work is organized in the community offers many new ideas for organizational research. The organizational concepts that would be worth studying are virtuality, temporariness, trust, reputation and cooperation. The open source model might also be used to reconsider consolidated organizational models from new points of view.

The way in which activities are carried out by members of the open source community could provide input for considering how work is organized. In particular, characteristics worth studying are the concepts of mobility, flexibility, autonomy, creativity and satisfaction.

An important area of research would be how the open source logic can be extended to other contexts. How and to what degree can open source principles be transferred to other industries and in particular to other categories of products and services?

The diffusion of the open source logic could have significant effects from a social point of view, especially if this is accompanied by a progressive strengthening of a culture or philosophy based on openness and cooperation and their social value.

I can only hope that many of the considerations in this book can open the way to new research aimed at investigating and evaluating the evolution of the open source phenomenon and its potential impacts not only on the ICT industry but on other industries and society as a whole.

References

[1] Stallman, R. (1999). The GNU Operating System and the Free Software Movement, in Di Bona, C. *et al.*, *Open Sources: Voices from the Open Source Revolution*.

[2] Torvalds, L. (1999). The Linux Edge, in Di Bona, C. *et al.*, *Open Sources: Voices from the Open Source Revolution*.

[3] http://www.opensource.org/halloween.

[4] http://www.netlingo.com/lookup.cfm?term=operating%20system.

[5] Stallman, R. (1999). The GNU Operating System and the Free Software Movement, in Di Bona, C. *et al.*, *Open Sources: Voices from the Open Source Revolution*.

[6] http://www.gnu.org/copyleft/gpl.html.

[7] Torvalds, L. (1999). Linux History, at http://www.li.org/li/linuxhistory.html.

[8] ibidem.

[9] Tuomi, I. (2001). Internet, Innovation, and Open Source: Actors in the Network, at http://www.firstmonday.org/issues/issue6_1/tuomi.

[10] http://www.redhat.com/about/corporate/milestones.html.

[11] http://en.wikipedia.org/wiki/Apache_Software_Foundation.

[12] http://www.opensource.org.

[13] Perens, B. (1999). The Open Source Definition, at http://opensource.org/docs/definition_plain.

[14] Hamerly, J. *et al.* (1999). Freeing the Source: The Story of Mozilla, in Di Bona, C. *et al.*, *Open Sources: Voices from the Open Source Revolution.*

[15] Ibidem.

[16] http://www.newsforge.com/print.pl?sid=04/07/19/2315200.

[17] Silver, J. (2003). What is Intellectual Property?: Trade Secret Law, at http://library.findlaw.com/2003/May/15/132743.html.

[18] http://media.wiley.com/product_data/excerpt/03/04712505/0471250503.pdf.

[19] http://www.european-patent-office.org/legal/epc/e/ar52.html#A52.

[20] Stallman, R. (2000). The Anatomy of a Trivial Patent, at http://lpf.ai.mit.edu/Patents/anatomy-trivial-patent.txt.

[21] Garfinkel, S. L., Stallman, R. M and Kapor, M. (1991). Against Software Patents, at http://lpf.ai.mit.edu/Patents/against-software-patents.html.
Garfinkel, S. L., Stallman, R. M and Kapor, M. (1991). Why Patents Are Bad for Software, at http://lpf.ai.mit.edu/Links/prep.ai.mit.edu/issues.article.

[22] Battilana, M. C. (2004). The GIF Controversy: A Software Developer's Perspective, at http://cloanto.com/users/mcb/19950127giflzw.html.

[23] http://www.gnu.org/licenses/licenses.html#WhatIsCopyleft.

[24] http://www.gnu.org/licenses/licenses.html#WhatIsCopyleft.

[25] Stallman, R. (2002). What Is Copyleft?, at http://www.fsf.org/copyleft/copyleft.html.
Stallman, R. (2002). Linux and the GNU Project, at http://www.gnu.org/gnu/linux-and-gnu.html.

[26] http://perens.com/Articles/OSD.html.

[27] Bessen, J. and Maskin, E. (2000). Sequential Innovation, Patents, and Imitation. Working Paper, Department of Economics, MIT.

[28] Vetter, G. (2004). The Collaborative Integrity of Open Source Software, *Utah Law Review*.

[29] Gates, W. (2001). Open Letter to Hobbyists, 3/2/1976, in Moody G., *Rebel Code*, Perseus.

[30] Torvalds, L. (1999). Linux History, at http://www.li.org/li/linuxhistory.html.

[31] Weber, S. (2000). The Political Economy of Open Source Software, *BRIE E-economy Project*, Berkeley, Working Paper 140.
Lerner, J. and Tirole, J. (2001). Some Simple Economics of Open Source, *Journal of Industrial Economics*, Vol. 50, pp. 197-234.
Tzouris, M. (2002). Software Freedom, Open Software and the Participant's Motivation. A Multidisciplinary Study, The London School of Economics and Political Science.
Bonaccorsi, A. and Rossi, C. (2002). Why Open Source Software Can Succeed?, Laboratory of Economy and Management, Sant'Anna School of Advanced Study, Pisa.

[32] Raymond, E. S. (1998). The Cathedral and the Bazaar, *First Monday*, Vol. 3, N. 3.

[33] Raymond, E. S (1999). The Magic Cauldron, at http://www.catb.org/~esr/writings/magic-cauldron/magic-cauldron.html.

[34] Feller, J. and Fitzgerald, B. (2002). *Understanding Opensource Software Development*, Addison-Wesley, London.

[35] McKelvey, M. (2001). Internet Entrepreneurship: Linux and the Dynamics of Open Source Software, *CRIC Discussion Paper*, N. 44, University of Manchester & UMIST.

[36] Ryan, R. M. and Deci, E. L. (2000). Self-Determination Theory and the Facilitation of Intrinsic Motivation, Social Development, and Well-Being, *American Psychologist*, 55, pp. 68-78.

[37] Hars, A. and Ou, S. (2001). Working for Free? Motivations for Participating in Open Source Projects, in Sprague, R. (Ed.), *Proceedings 34th HICSS Conference*.
Hertel, G., Niedner, S. and Hermann, S. (2003). Motivation of Software Developers in the Open Source Projects: An Internet-Based Survey of Contributors to the Linux Kernel, *Research Policy*, 32(7), pp. 1159-1177.
Lakhani, K. and Wolf, R. (2001). Does Free Software Mean Free Labor? Characteristics of Participants in Open Source Communities, *Boston Consulting Group Survey Report*, Boston, MA.

[38] Lakhani, K. R. and Von Hippel, E. (2002). How Open Source Software Works: Free User-to-User Assistance, Cambridge, MIT Sloan School of Management.
Bonaccorsi, A. and Rossi, C. (2002). Why Open Source Software Can Succeed?, Laboratory of Economy and Management, Sant'Anna School of Advanced Study, Pisa.

[39] Diamond, D., Torvalds, L. (2001). *Just for Fun: The Story of an Accidental Revolutionary*, Harper Business, New York, NY, USA.

[40] Hars, A. and Ou, S. (2001). Working for Free? Motivations for Participating in Open Source Projects, in Sprague, R. (Ed.), *Proceedings 34th HICSS Conference*.
Lakhani, K. and Wolf R. (2001). Does Free Software Mean Free Labor? Characteristics of Participants in Open Source Communities, *Boston Consulting Group Survey Report*, Boston, MA.

[41] Raymond, E. S. (1998). Homesteading the Noosphere, *First Monday*, Vol. 3, N. 10.
Lancashire, D. (2001). Coding, Culture and Cash: The Fading Altruism of Open Source Development, *First Monday*, Vol. 6, N. 12.

[42] Graham, P. quoted by Vetter, G. R. (2004). The Collaborative Integrity of Open Source Software, *Utah Law Review*, p. 563.

[43] Raymond, E. S. (1998). The Cathedral and the Bazaar, *First Monday,* Vol. 3, N. 3.

[44] Barbrook, R. (1998). The Hi-Tech Gift Economy, *First Monday*, Vol. 3, N. 12.

Bergquist, M. and Ljungberg, J. (2001). The Power of Gifts: Organizing Social Relationships in Open Source Communities, *Information Systems Journal*, Vol. 11, pp. 305-320.

Iannacci, F. (2002). *The Economics of Open-Source Networks*, London School of Economics, Department of Information Systems.

[45] Kuwabara, K. (2000). Linux: A Bazaar at the Edge of Chaos, *First Monday*, Vol. 5, N. 3.

"[...] *those who create the greatest amounts of information obtain status"* Raymond, E. S. (1998). Homesteading the Noosphere, *First Monday,* Vol. 3, N. 10.

[46] Raymond, E. S. (1998). Homesteading the Noosphere, *First Monday,* Vol. 3, N. 10.

[47] Dafermos, G. N. (2001). Management and Virtual Decentralised Networks: The Linux Project, *First Monday*, Vol. 6, N. 11.

Bonaccorsi, A. and Rossi, C. (2002). Why Open Source Software Can Succeed?, Laboratory of Economics and Management, Sant'Anna School of Advanced Study, Pisa.

[48] Jørgensen, N. (2001). Putting it All in the Trunk: Incremental Software Development in the FreeBSD Open Source Project, *Information Systems Journal*, Vol. 11, pp. 321-336.

[49] Brooks, F. (1975). *The Mythical Man Month: Essays on Software Engineering*, London, Addison-Wesley.

[50] Raymond, E. S. (1998). The Cathedral and the Bazaar, *First Monday,* Vol. 3, N. 3.

Lerner, J. and Tirole, J. (2001). Some Simple Economics of Open Source, *Journal of Industrial Economics*, Vol. 50, pp. 197-234.

[51] Sommerville, I. (1999). *Software Engineering*, Pearson Education.
Scacchi, W. (2001). Process Models in Software Engineering, at
http://www.ics.uci.edu/~wscacchi/Papers/SE-Encyc/Process-Models-SE-
Encyc.pdf.

[52] Sommerville, I. (1999). *Software Engineering*, Pearson Education.

[53] Scacchi, W. (2001). Process Models in Software Engineering.

[54] Boehm, B. W. (1988). A Spiral Model of Software Development and
Enhancement, at
http://www.computer.org/computer/homepage/misc/Boehm/r5061.pdf.
Pfleeger, S. L. (2000). *Software Engineering: Theory and Practice*, Prentice
Hall.
Vliet, H. (1999). *Software Engineering: Principles and Practice*, Wiley.

[55] Scacchi, W. (2001). Process Models in Software Engineering, Institute for
Software Research, University of California, Irvine, in Marciniak, J. J. (Ed.)
(2001), *Encyclopedia of Software Engineering, 2nd Edition*, John Wiley and
Sons, Inc, New York.

[56] Cusumano, M. A. and Selby, R. W. (1995). *Microsoft Secrets: How the
World's Most Powerful Software Company Creates Technology, Shapes
Markets, and Manages People*, Free Press.
Yoffie, D. B. (1997). *Competing in the Age of Digital Convergence*, Harvard
Business School Press.

[57] *"[...] the basic idea is that user needs for many types of software are so
difficult to understand that is nearly impossible or unwise to try to design the
system completely in advance, especially as hardware improvements and
customer desires are constantly and quickly evolving. Instead project should
iterate as well as concurrently manage as many design, build, and testing
activities as possible while they move forward to complete a product."*
Cusumano and Selby, (1995). *Microsoft Secrets*.

[58] Cusumano, M. A. and Selby, R. W. (1995). *Microsoft Secrets: How the
World's Most Powerful Software Company Creates Technology, Shapes
Markets, and Manages People*, Free Press.

[59] Asundi, J. (2001). Software Engineering Lessons from Open Source Projects, at http://opensource.ucc.ie/icse2001/asundi.pdf.

[60] Garcia, M. J. (2001). Innovating Without Money: Linux and the Open Source Paradigm as an Alternative to Commercial Software Development, at http://opensource.mit.edu/papers/mateos.pdf.
Zhao, L. and Elbaum, S. (2003). Quality assurance under the open source development model, *Journal of Systems and Software,* Volume 66, N. 1.
Franke, N. and Hippel, E. (2002). Satisfying Heterogeneous User Needs via Innovation Toolkits: The Case of Apache Security Software, at http://userinnovation.mit.edu/papers/1.pdf.

[61] http://www.freshmeat.net.

[62] ISO 8402, at http://www.iso.org.

[63] Moller, K. and Paulish, D. (1993). *Software Metrics,* Chapman & Hall.
Spiller, D. and Wichmann, T. (2002). *Free/Libre and Open Source Software: Survey and Study,* Part 3: Basics of Open Source Software Markets and Business Models, Berlecon Research, Berlin.

[64] Weinberg, G. M. (1991). *Quality Software Management,* Dorset House Publishing Company.
Pearson, M. J. *et al.* (1995). Total Quality Management: Are Information Systems Managers Ready?, *Information & Management,* Vol. 29, N. 5, pp. 251-263.
Parzinger, M. and Nath, R. (2000). A Study of the Relationship Between Total Quality Management Implementation Factors and Software Quality, *Total Quality Management,* Vol. 11, N. 3, pp. 353-371.

[65] Arthur, L. J. (1993). *Improving Software Quality: An Insider's Guide to TQM,* Wiley.

[66] Software Engineering Institute (1993). Capability Maturity Model for Software, Version 1.1, at http://www.sei.cmu.edu/cmm/.

[67] Humphrey, W. S. (1988). Characterizing the Software Process: A Maturity Framework, *IEEE Software,* pp. 73-79.

[68] Software Engineering Institute (1993). Capability Maturity Model for Software, Version 1.1, at http://www.sei.cmu.edu/cmm/.

[69] Wheeler, D. A. (2005). Why Open Source Software / Free Software (OSS/FS, FLOSS, or FOSS)? Look at the Numbers!, at http://dwheeler.com/oss_fs_why.html.

[70] http://www.spec.org/.

[71] IDA now IDABC Interoperable Delivery of European eGovernment Services to Public Administrations, Businesses and Citizens, at http://europa.eu.int/idabc/.

[72] Moschella, D. C. (1997). *Waves of Power: Dynamics of Global Technology Leadership*, American Management Association.

[73] Yoffie, D. B. (1997). *Competing in the Age of Digital Convergence*, Harvard Business School Press.
Chesbrough, H. W. and Teece, D. J. (1996). When is Virtual Virtuous? Organizing for Innovation, *Harvard Business Review*, Jan-Feb.

[74] Shapiro, C. and Varian H. L. (1998). *Information Rules: A Strategic Guide to the Network Economy*, Harvard Business School Press.
Teece D.J., (1986). Profiting from Technological Innovation: Implication for Integration, Collaboration, Licensing and Public Policy, *Research Policy*, Vol. 15, pp. 285-305.

[75] Valloppillil, V. (1998). Open Source Software: A (New?) Development Methodology, at http://www.opensource.org/halloween/halloween1.html
West, J. (2002). How Open is Open Enough? Melding Proprietary and Open Source Platform Strategies, at http://opensource.mit.edu/papers/rp-west.pdf.

[76] Shapiro, C. and Varian, H. L. (1998). *Information Rules: A Strategic Guide to the Network Economy*, Harvard Business School Press.

[77] Kelly, K. (1998). *New Rules for the New Economy: 10 Radical Strategies for a Connected World*, Penguin.

Katz, M. and Shapiro, C. (1985). Network Externality, Competition and Compatibility, *American Economic Review*, Vol. 75, N. 3, pp. 424-440.

[78] Arthur, B. W. (1990). Positive Feedbacks in the Economy, *Scientific American*, Vol. 262, pp. 92-99.

Arthur, B.W. (1996). Increasing Returns and the New World of Business, *Harvard Business Review*, July/August.

[79] David, P. (1985). CLIO and the Economics of QWERTY, *American Economic Review*, Vol. 75, pp. 332-337.

Teece, D. J. (1986). Profiting from Technological Innovation: Implication for Integration, Collaboration, Licensing and Public Policy, *Research Policy*, Vol. 15, pp. 285-305.

Rosenbloom, R. S. and Cusumano, M. A. (1987). Technological Pioneering and Competitive Advantage: The Birth of the VCR industry, *California Management Review*, Vol. 29, N. 4.

Shapiro, C. and Varian, H. L. (1998). *Information Rules: A Strategic Guide to the Network Economy*, Harvard Business School Press.

[80] Perens, B. *et al.*, Free Software Leaders Stand Together, at http://perens.com/Articles/StandTogether.html.

[81] Catania, E. (2003). Interview, Corriere della Sera, 3 February.

[82] http://www.zdnet.com.au/news/software/0,2000061733,39149502,00.htm.

[83] Raymond, E. (1999). The Magic Cauldron, at http://www.catb.org/~esr/writings/magic-cauldron/magic-cauldron.html#toc3.

[84] Young, R. (1999). Giving It Away: How Red Hat Software Stumbled Across a New Economic Model and Helped Improve an Industry, in Di Bona, C. *et al.*, *Opensources: Voices from the Opensource Revolution*, Sebastol, O'Reilly & Associates.

[85] Hahn, R. W. (2002). *Government Policy toward Open Source Software*, AEI-Brookings Joint Center for Regulatory Studies, Washington D.C.

[86] *"In a sense, open source provision is an extension of the market, not an alternative."* Bessen, J. (2002). What Good is Free Software?, in Hahn, R. W. (2002), *Government Policy toward Open Source Software*, AEI-Brookings Joint Center for Regulatory Studies, Washington D.C.

[87] Evans, D. S. (2002). Politics and Programming: Government Preferences for Promoting Open Source Software, in Hahn, R. W. (200). *Government Policy toward Open Source Software*, AEI-Brookings Joint Center for Regulatory Studies, Washington D.C.

[88] *"[...] both open source and commercial software are integral parts of the broader software ecosystem. The open source and commercial models have coexisted within the software ecosystem for decades, and both have played important roles in its evolution. Moreover, recent actions by several leading software firms suggest that elements of these two models are beginning to overlap in important ways. Notably, this process is occurring solely in response to market forces and is not the result of law or regulation."*
"Only the marketplace, founded on a robust regime of property rights, can provide the combination of incentives and flexibility that will ensure not only that innovation occurs, but also that it proceeds in directions that satisfy actual market needs. While government intervention into the software marketplace may at times be necessary to correct specific instances of market failure, there is currently no such market failure that would justify regulatory preferences for open source software."
"[...] government could play a role in promoting software research under licensing terms that allow the results to be commercialized. [...] Governments should also ensure that the results of publicly funded research are not subject to licensing restrictions—such as those set out in the GNU General Public License (GPL) or similar "free" licenses—that would prevent industry from utilizing this research in commercial products. [...] Publicly funded research has played a critical factor in the success of the U.S. IT industry by helping to create a bedrock of technical knowledge that industry can then develop into commercially useful products. As long as such research is made available under terms that do not limit its utilization in commercial products, this research will be an extremely important resource for continued innovation in the software industry." Smith, B. (2002). The Future of Software: Enabling the Marketplace to Decide, in Hahn, R. W. (2002), *Government Policy toward Open Source Software*, AEI-Brookings Joint Center for Regulatory Studies, Washington D.C.

[89] http://www.berlios.de/index.php.en.

[90] http://www.sun.com/solutions/documents/articles/hc_brit_hth_aa.xml.

[91] http://www.softwarechoice.org/default.aspx.

[92] Rifkin, J. (2000). *The Age of Access: The New Culture of Hypercapitalism, Where All of Life Is a Paid-For Experience*, Putnam Publishing Group.

[93] Shenhar, A. and Dvir, D. (1996). Toward a Typological Theory of Project Management, *Research Policy*, Vol. 25, pp. 607-632.

[94] *"Work is what you do, not where you go."* Handy, C. (1995). Trust and the Virtual Corporation, *Harvard Business Review*, Vol. 73 , pp. 40-50.

[95] Rayport, J. F. and Sviokla, J. J. (1995*)*. Exploiting the Virtual Value Chain, *Harvard Business Review*, 73, pp. 75-85.
Giddens, A. (1990). *The Consequences of Modernity*, Stanford University Press, Stanford, CA.

[96] Handy, C. (1995). Trust and the Virtual Corporation, *Harvard Business Review*, Vol. 73, pp. 40-50.

[97] Becker, G. S. (1975). *Human Capital: A Theoretical and Empirical Analysis*, National Boureau of Economic Research, New York.
Coleman, J. S. (1988). Social Capital in the Creation of Human Capital, *American Journal of Sociology*, N. 94.
Putnam, R. D. (1993). The Prosperous Community: Social Capital and Public Life, *American Prospect*, N. 13, pp. 35-42.
Putnam, R. D. (1995). Bowling Alone: America's Declining Social Capital, *Journal of Democracy*, N. 6, pp. 65-78.

[98] Martin, J. (1992). *Cultures in Organizations: Three Perspectives*, Oxford University Press, New York.
Wiesenfeld, B. *et al.* (1998). Communication Patterns as Determinants of Organizational Identification in a Virtual Organization, *Journal of Computer Mediated Communication*, Vol. 3, N. 4.

Davidow, W. H. and Malone, M. S. (1992). *The Virtual Corporation: Structuring and Revitalizing the Corporation of the 21st Century*, Harper Collins, New York.

[99] Himanen, P. (2001). *The Hacker Ethic*, Random House.

[100] Castells, M. (1996). *The Rise of Network Society*, Blackwell.

[101] De Masi, D. (1995), *Il Futuro del lavoro. Fiducia e ozio nella società postindustriale*, Rizzoli (in Italian).
De Masi, D. (2000), *Ozio Creativo*, Rizzoli (in Italian).

[102] Burton-Jones, A. (1999). *Knowlegde Capitalism: Business, Work and Learning in the New Economy*, Oxford University Press.

[103] Pink, D. H. (2002). *Free Agents Nation: The Future of Working for Yourself*, Warner Books, New York.

[104] Reich, R. (2001). *The Future of Success, The Obsolescence of Loyalty and the Sale of the Self*, Alphred A Knopf, New York.

[105] Handy, C. (1990). *The Age of Unreason*, Harvard Business School Press.

[106] Amabile, T. (2002). Motivational Sinergy: Toward New Conceptualizations of Intrinsic and Extrinsic Motivation in the Workplace, *Human Resource Management Review*, Vol. 3, N. 3.
    Amabile, T. (1998). How to Kill Creativity, *Harvard Business Review*.
    Amabile, T. (1997). Motivating Creativity in the Organization: On Doing What You Love and Loving What You Do, *California Management Review*, Vol. 40, N. 1.

[107] Csikszentmihalyi, M. (1996). *Creativity Flow and the Psycology of Discovery and Invention*, Happer Collins.
    Csikszentmihalyi, M. (1992). *The Psychology of Happiness*, Harper and Row.

[108] Amabile, T. (1997). Motivating Creativity in the Organization: On Doing What You Love and Loving What You Do, *California Management Review*, Vol. 40, N. 1.

Amabile, T. *et al.* (2002). Creativity under the Gun, *Harvard Business Review*.

[109] Florida, R. (2002). *The Rise of the Creative Class and How it is Transforming Work, Leisure, Community, and Everyday Life*, Basic Book, New York.

[110] Himanen, P. (2001). *The Hacker Ethic*, Random House.

[111] Raymond, E. S. (2003). *The Art of Unix Programming*, Addison-Wesley.

[112] Rifkin, J. (1995). *The End of Work: The Decline of the Global Labor Force and the Dawn of the Post-Market Era*, Putnam Publishing Group.

[113] Putnam, R. D. (1995). Bowling Alone: America's Declining Social Capital, *Journal of Democracy*, N. 6, pp. 65-78.

[114] Axelrod, R. and Cohen, M. D. (1999). *Harnessing Complexity: Organizational Implications of a Scientific Frontier*, The Free Press, New York.

[115] ibidem.

[116] Waldrop, M. M. (1992). *Complexity: The Emerging Science at the Edge of Order and Chaos*, Simon & Schuster, New York.
Kelly, K. (1994). *Out of Control: The New Biology of Machines, Social Systems, and the Economic World*, Addison-Wesley, Reading, MA.
Lissack, M. R. (1999). Complexity: The Science, its Vocabulary, and its Relation to Organizations, *Emergence*, Vol. 1, N.1, pp. 110-126.
McKelvey, B. (1999). Complexity Theory in Organization Science: Seizing the Promise or Becoming a Fad?, *Emergence*, Vol. 1, N.1, pp. 5-32.
Coleman, J. H. Jr. (1999). What Enables Self-Organizing Behavior in Businesses, *Emergence*, Vol. 1, N. 1, pp. 33-48.

[117] ibidem.

[118] Lerner, J. and Tirole, J. (2001). Some Simple Economics of Open Source, *Journal of Industrial Economics*, Vol. 50, pp. 197-234.

[119] Axelrod, R. and Cohen, M. D. (1999). *Harnessing Complexity: Organizational Implications of a Scientific Frontier*, The Free Press, New York.
McKelvey, B. (1999). Complexity Theory in Organization Science: Seizing the Promise or Becoming a Fad?, *Emergence*, Vol. 1, N. 1, pp. 5-32.

[120] http://en.wikipedia.org/wiki/Free_rider.html.

[121] Raymond, E. S. (1998). The Cathedral and the Bazaar, *First Monday*, Vol. 3, N. 3.

[122] Benkler, Y. (2001). Coase's Penguin, or, Linux and the Nature of the Firm, at http://www.benkler.org/CoasesPenguin.pdf.

[123] Why Open Content Matters, *Linux Journal*, 11 April 2001.

[124] http://ocw.mit.edu/index.html.

[125] Ishii, K. and Lutterbeck, B. (2001). Unexploited Resources of Online Education for Democracy — Why the Future Should Belong to OpenCourseWare, *First Monday*, Vol. 6, N. 11.

[126] http://www.promo.net/pg/.

[127] http://dmoz.org/about.html.

[128] http://slashdot.org.

[129] http://bioinformatics.org.

[130] Lessig, L. (2001). *The Future of Ideas: The Fate of the Commons in a Connected World*, Ramdom House.

[131] http://www.rattlesnake.com/intro/Free-Software-and-Free-Manuals.html.

[132] http://www.gnu.org/licenses/licenses.html#FDL.

[133] http://creativecommons.org/learn/aboutus/.

[134] Ibidem.

[135] http://science.creativecommons.org/.

[136] http://www.publiclibraryofscience.org/.

[137] http://www.plos.org/about/history.html.

[138] http://artlibre.org/licence.php/lalgb.html.

[139] http://cyber.law.harvard.edu/openlaw/.

[140] http://www.eff.org/about/#who.

[141] Gabriel, R. P. and Goldman, R. (2002). Open Source: Beyond the Fairytales, at http://opensource.mit.edu/papers/gabrielgoldman.pdf.